Praise for *Anchore*

"Presenting Stephen Porges's justly celebrated Polyvagal Theory in clear and concise language for the layperson, Deb Dana guides us, by means of simple exercises, to understand and befriend our autonomic nervous system, engaging its healing capacities to connect with ourselves and with our social world."

GABOR MATÉ, MD
author of *In the Realm of Hungry Ghosts*

"Master trauma therapist and clinical trainer Deb Dana is already well-known and deeply appreciated for the deftness of her translations of obtuse science—neuroception and autonomic hierarchy—into accessible common sense. We work with **S**tories, **A**ctions, **F**eelings, and **E**mbodied sensations to come home to safety, connection, and well-being. In *Anchored*, she radically—and masterfully—shifts the entire focus of our current paradigms of healing and growth to a new vocabulary and new practices for regulating the (re)activity of the human nervous system that underlies all of our personal struggles and the stories we tell ourselves about them. Deb offers a wealth of very doable explorations and practices for noticing, befriending, shifting, and shaping our automatic responses to cues of safety and danger, and she leads us through vivid examples and the practical explorations that reliably lead us home to safety, connection, and well-being. We can all be grateful for the wise guidance that is the *Anchored* road map."

LINDA GRAHAM, MFT
author of *Resilience*

"*Anchored* is a beautiful, almost lyrical guide to befriending our nervous system in ways that allow us to immerse ourselves more fully in the mysterious wonders of living and loving. Deb Dana has elegantly translated neuroscience into everyday words and experiences that illustrate how we move in and out of states of safe connection and states of protecting ourselves, guided by our wondrously complex and adaptive nervous system. Full of examples and simple, clear exercises, this lovely book gently supports a growing curiosity and awareness of the subtle shifts in our bodies as our nervous system reflects old stories and creates new ones about who we are and how we move through the world. Readers from all walks of life will find this an accessible and practical book for recognizing and understanding patterns of protection that hold us back, and for learning how to regularly (re)anchor ourselves in deep loving and living."

KATHY STEELE, MN, CS
coauthor of *Treating Trauma-Related Dissociation*

ANCHORED

ALSO BY DEB DANA

The Polyvagal Theory in Therapy:
Engaging the Rhythm of Regulation

Polyvagal Exercises for Safety and Connection:
50 Client-Centered Practices

Polyvagal Flip Chart: Understanding the Science of Safety

Clinical Applications of the Polyvagal Theory: The Emergence
of Polyvagal-Informed Therapies (with Stephen W. Porges)

Befriending Your Nervous System:
Looking Through the Lens of Polyvagal Theory

foreword by *Stephen W. Porges, PhD*

DEB DANA

ANCHORED

*How to Befriend Your Nervous System
Using Polyvagal Theory*

sounds true
BOULDER, COLORADO

PVI | polyvagal institute
the art and science of human connection

Published 2021

Cover design by Tara DeAngelis
Book design by Meredith March

FSC
www.fsc.org
MIX
Paper | Supporting
responsible forestry
FSC® C103098

Self-Compassion Break practice on page 30 republished with permission of Guilford
Publications, Inc., from *The Mindful Self-Compassion Workbook: A Proven Way to Accept
Yourself, Build Inner Strength, and Thrive* by Kristin Neff and Christopher Germer, 2018.
Permission conveyed through Copyright Clearance Center, Inc.

"This Urge for Here," "After a Blizzard" (excerpt), and "Startled by Earth" (excerpt) are from
Having Listened by Gary Whited, Homebound Publications, 2013. Used with permission.

Printed in the United States of America

BK06090

Library of Congress Cataloging-in-Publication Data

Names: Dana, Deb, author.
Title: Anchored : how to befriend your nervous system using polyvagal theory /
  Deborah A. Dana, LCSW; foreword by Stephen Porges, PhD.
Description: Boulder, CO : Sounds True, 2021. | Includes bibliographical references.
Identifiers: LCCN 2020058084 (print) | LCCN 2020058085 (ebook) |
  ISBN 9781683647065 (paperback) | ISBN 9781683647072 (ebook)
Subjects: LCSH: Autonomic nervous system. | Psychic trauma–Treatment. |
  Affective neuroscience.
Classification: LCC QP368 .D356 2021 (print) | LCC QP368 (ebook) | DDC
  612.8/1–dc23
LC record available at https://lccn.loc.gov/2020058084
LC ebook record available at https://lccn.loc.gov/2020058085

To my polyvagal family

CONTENTS

FOREWORD

by Stephen W. Porges, PhD

As I read *Anchored*, I recognized that Deb Dana has made an important contribution by providing a powerful metaphor to illustrate how the nervous system regulates its resources to provide a neural platform for social behavior and gain the benefits of co-regulation. In *Anchored*, Deb shares her intellectual and insightful gifts by translating the complex neurophysiological constructs embedded in Polyvagal Theory into accessible language. As she links words to visualizations and visualization to bodily feelings, her gifts go well beyond linguistic skills and effectively bring bodily feelings into awareness. Through this strategy, Deb teaches the reader of *Anchored* the skills to move safely back into their body.

From a polyvagal perspective, Deb artfully and efficiently leads readers through structured neural exercises that effectively enable their nervous systems to more efficiently support homeostatic functions, leading to health, growth, and restoration. Or, more succinctly stated, she outlines neural exercises that will provide resources to downregulate threats and enable spontaneous social engagement, which in combination create a fluid path toward co-regulation and embodiment. The product of this strategy is a more resilient nervous system that supports both mental and physical health.

In reading *Anchored*, I became focused on the parallel between the communication strategies within the body and among individuals. These are interdependent levels of co-regulation, since a regulated and resourced nervous system spontaneously downregulates defensive reactions, while a nervous system in chronic states of threat downregulates opportunities to socially engage. Fortunately, through our evolutionary history, we as social mammals have developed a portal to downregulate our threat reactions through the neuroception of safety. However, access to this portal is greatly influenced by the neural state of the individual. If the autonomic nervous system is well resourced, we are resilient and there is a low threshold to trigger states of safety that would lead to spontaneous social engagement and co-regulation. Alternately, if we are locked into a defensive state, feelings of safety may not be easily accessible.

The title *Anchored* serves as a metaphor that Deb brilliantly uses to create the visualization of a safe place within the individual's concept of their personal resources (e.g., nervous system, concept of self). This serves them on their personal journey of embodiment with the attributes of resilience, self-regulation within, and co-regulation with others.

Functionally, the journey requires us to, first, become aware of the neurophysiological circuits involved in feelings of safety, danger, and life threat; second, become aware of the power of neuroception, the detection of cues of threat and safety without conscious awareness; and third, through visualizations and experientials, become of aware of the shifts in autonomic state. As a package, this sequence can be conceptualized as neural exercises, which would promote greater self-awareness and self-regulation, leading to greater resilience.

In a recent paper, I framed the Polyvagal Theory as a scientific extrapolation of the phylogenetic journey toward sociality functionally expressed in social mammals, which evolved from asocial reptiles. Through this journey, the neurophysiological portal to sociality required an efficient mechanism to detect safety and to reflexively downregulate defense. Basically, the neural mechanisms underlying sociality enable the rapid transition from aggressive or submissive threat reactions to a physiology that enables accessibility and promotes opportunities to co-regulate. As a scientist and the creator of the Polyvagal Theory, my narrative describing and justifying the theory continues to evolve. Although the world of trauma therapy rapidly grasped the importance of the theory as it related to the experiences of their clients, I was slower in grasping the significance of the theory in the treatment of trauma and other mental health–related disorders. I had to learn from therapists and their clients, who informed me of the value of the theory both in clinical practice and in transforming the personal narrative of trauma survivors.

Deb Dana is one of these insightful and articulate therapists who has informed me about the role Polyvagal Theory can play both in the clinical process and in everyday social interactions. Deb rapidly embraced the theory and, through her unique insights and communication skills, made the theory more accessible not only to therapists but as a map to understanding our personal roles in our daily social interactions. Deb expressed in her work that it is the bodily feelings and not the events that are central to the experience of trauma. Her work focuses on the central theme through which Polyvagal Informed Therapies function.

Polyvagal Informed Therapies shift the focus of therapy from the traumatic event to the bodily feeling. This is an important theoretical transformation about how trauma is both treated and embedded in the survivor's nervous system. On the foundational level, Polyvagal Theory emphasizes that physiological state forms the intervening variable that determines our reactivity to cues and contexts. Thus, the theory emphasizes that it is not trauma as an event that is the primary determinant of outcome. Rather, the theory emphasizes that it is the re-tuning of the neural regulation of the autonomic nervous system to support threat reactions that is the primary determinant of outcome. This does not preclude the importance of the traumatic event but acknowledges the great individual differences in outcomes to common traumatic experiences. The Polyvagal perspective of trauma differs from the focus of epidemiological research, which emphasizes scales such as the Adverse Childhood Experiences (ACEs) and the identification of specific events as causal in the conceptualization of PTSD. This strategy redefines the trauma and moves it from being within the individual to an external event.

Prevalent contemporary epidemiological models assume that the relevant events can be quantitatively evaluated along a continuum of severity of trauma, stress, or abuse. However, Polyvagal Theory shifts the dialogue from the external event to the intervening neural system that can be vulnerable or resilient to threat. If the individual is in a vulnerable state, then lower intensity events can disrupt neural function and shift the nervous system from a state supporting homeostasis to a vulnerable state reflecting autonomic destabilization with consequential comorbidities. If the system is resilient, it can functionally buffer the impact of higher intensity events. The theory suggests that a profound retuning of the autonomic nervous system following the traumatic event is an adaptive consequence of surviving trauma.

To tap in to this intervening variable in survey research, we created the Body Perception Questionnaire (BPQ). The BPQ is a relatively short questionnaire that evaluates the reactivity of our autonomic nervous system. The psychometrics are well established, and several studies have been published using the scale. (The scale and scoring information are available on my webpage, stephenporges.com.) In my colleague's and my research, we documented the profound role of autonomic regulation as an intervening variable mediating the impact of adversity history. We found that if adults with an adversity history also had an autonomic nervous system tuned to be threat reactive, their outcomes were worse. This was confirmed by two recently published studies: one investigating sexual function and the other exploring mental health reactions during the pandemic.

This emphasis on sociality transforms Polyvagal Theory into a clinically relevant perspective. When the initial tenants of the theory were introduced more than twenty-five years ago, application in basic medicine was more central to the theory than mental health was. I thought the theory would have traction in obstetrics, neonatology, pediatrics, cardiology, and other medical specialties concerned with atypical autonomic function. As I listen to Deb and am informed about her applications and insights, Polyvagal Theory takes on new meanings in the understanding and treatment of mental *and* physical health. As we embrace the core message of the theory that we are a social species without the accessibility of our mammalian heritage, we recognize we lack the neural resources to be safe and to co-regulate with others. This heritage pivots on two uniquely mammalian features: one, a neuroception process that enables the downregulation of defense states through reflexive detection of cues of safety; and two, a neural circuit, the ventral vagal complex, with its capacity to both calm defenses and provide cues of safety via an integrated social engagement system. This heritage links behavior and psychological experience with definable and measurable neurophysiological mechanisms, a link that joins mental and physical health and dispels myths of their independence.

Anchored focuses on the bold therapeutic problem of how to return to the safety of our body. *Anchored* is about getting reacquainted with bodily feelings without the familiar embedded associations of these feelings with dangerous events. By establishing a secure anchor within the body, we can safely explore feelings that would previously be destabilizing. Having an anchor provides the stability to explore and safely feel the wounds still held in the body. This process supports the journey of healing in which the nervous system will become sufficiently resilient to engage others and find humor and excitement, not threat, while navigating a complex and often unpredictable world. In *Anchored*, Deb has mastered a language that allows all of us, regardless of education and profession, to experience overt actions and covert visualizations as efficient neural exercises to metaphorically follow the cable leading to internal feelings of safety that are now anchored within the nervous system.

INTRODUCTION

Polyvagal Theory is the science of feeling safe enough
to fall in love with life and take the risks of living.

We are wired for connection. Our nervous systems are social structures that find balance and stability in relationship with others. Think about that for a moment. Our biology shapes the way we navigate living, loving, and working. And we now have a way to use this understanding in service of individual, family, community, and global well-being. This "way" is called Polyvagal Theory. Polyvagal Theory was first developed in the 1990s by Stephen Porges. It explains the science of connection, offering a map of the nervous system to guide our exploration as well as skills we can practice to strengthen our ability to anchor ourselves and each other in safety and regulation in the midst of challenges to our sense of equilibrium.

Since 2014, I have collaborated with Dr. Porges as a mentor, coauthor, colleague, and friend and have been actively translating the science of Polyvagal Theory into clinical application. With this book, I hope to translate Polyvagal Theory even further so that anyone can have access to its core concepts and experience its many benefits for living and navigating life with greater ease.

Even with this translation, there is some new terminology to learn. While words like *neuroception, hierarchy, ventral vagal, sympathetic,* and *dorsal vagal* may seem daunting at first, I'll help you become fluent in the basic vocabulary and get comfortable in speaking the language of the nervous system. You'll see in the chapters that follow that I sometimes substitute the words *safe, connected,* or *regulating* for *ventral vagal; mobilized* or *fight and flight* for *sympathetic;* and *disconnected, shut down,* or *collapsed* for *dorsal.* As you begin to befriend your nervous system, you'll have the opportunity to find your own words.

The human autonomic nervous system evolved over many millennia and is based on a universal design that is a common denominator across human experience. Called *autonomic* as a reference to the autonomous, automatic way it functions, this system regulates internal organs and body processes including heartbeat, breath rhythms, blood pressure, digestion, and metabolism. The role of the autonomic nervous system is to store, conserve, and release energy to help us safely move through our daily lives.

This system works in predictable ways, and this shared experience brings us together. Looking through the lens of the nervous system, we understand that we are all trying to anchor in the state of safety that supports connection to self, to others, to the world, and to spirit and provides the energy we need to navigate our days. When the inner workings of our biology are a mystery, we feel as if we're at the mercy of unknown, unexplainable, and unpredictable experiences. Once we know how our nervous system works, we can work with it. As we learn the art of befriending our nervous system, we learn to become active operators of this essential system.

A regulated nervous system is fundamental to the process of navigating the world with a sense of safety and ease. We all encounter problems over the course of a day. Some are more easily managed than others, but no matter where an experience lands on the continuum of mild to traumatic, understanding how the nervous system works is the path to finding the way back to regulation. When we learn to befriend the nervous system, track states, and anchor in autonomic safety, the inevitable challenges that we all face as we go through our days aren't quite so formidable. If we put a problem aside and turn our attention toward learning how to shape our systems in the direction of safety and connection, we can return to the problem and see it in a new way. Anchored in a regulated system, options appear and possibilities emerge.

How to Use This Book

Our stories about who we are and how we see the world begin in our bodies. Before the brain can assemble thoughts and language, the nervous system initiates a response that moves us toward an experience and into connection, takes us into the mobilizing protection of fight and flight, or rescues us through shutdown and disconnection.

How do we begin to befriend this system? How do we learn to tune in and turn toward the important information our nervous system holds and use this information to be active authors of our personal stories? Mindfully meeting the autonomic nervous system begins with understanding the way this system works and creating skill in following the moment-to-moment flow between action, withdrawal, and connection. With that awareness we can bring in practices to gently shape the system in new ways and enjoy the sense of ease that comes from living with a nervous system that responds with flexibility to the ordinary—and sometimes extraordinary—challenges we meet each day.

The chapters in this book offer small steps that help you befriend your nervous system. The experiential practices build from one chapter to the next in an order designed to keep the process from feeling overwhelming. Each chapter offers practices, labeled "explorations," to bring the theory portion into an embodied experience. After you've completed the book, you can go back and re-read chapters and return to the explorations. They are offered so you can experiment as you go and then come back to the ones that help you feel a sense of well-being and make them part of an ongoing practice. Many of the explorations include a suggestion to document what you find and want to remember. I chose the word *document* to invite the use of both words and images. At times you may find that a single word or several bullet points help you hold on to the new information, while at other times you may decide a longer piece of writing or illustrations and color may be how you want to record what is important. Each invitation to document is an invitation to choose how you want to remember and revisit what you discovered.

Throughout the chapters of the book, you'll learn about the basic principles of Polyvagal Theory and then bring the science into everyday application with explorations that bring the theory alive. My hope is that when you've finished the book, you'll move through the world in a new way and experience the powerful benefits that come with finding your personal pathways to calm and connection.

This process of befriending the nervous system is an ongoing journey of discovery. I have been exploring this territory for a long time and have wisdom and expertise to share. And just like you I'm still challenged by daily experiences and find myself in moments of messiness, moments when I lose my anchor in my state of what is known as "ventral vagal safety and regulation." When that happens, I need to remember what I know and put it back into practice.

The title of this book, *Anchored*, is a word you'll hear repeated throughout the chapters. I grew up around the water, understanding how anchors are essential to staying safe in response to changing conditions. An anchor digs into the ocean floor with enough line between it and the boat to hold the boat safely in one place but with enough leeway to move in response to changes in the sea and wind. Safety comes with a firmly embedded anchor and the right amount of line. When we are anchored, we have a sense of being safely held so we can venture out without becoming adrift. We are connected to a state of regulation and have room to explore the world around us.

When I offered my first clinical training, I told the participants they were being welcomed into the polyvagal family that was emerging from my collaboration with Dr. Porges. That polyvagal family has grown into a global polyvagal community, but the feeling is still very much one of family. As you begin this book, I'm extending an invitation to join this growing polyvagal family and find a new language of human connection.

1

A Quick Look at the
Principles and Elements
of Polyvagal Theory

The beauty of a living thing is not the atoms that go
into it, but the way those atoms are put together.
CARL SAGAN,
COSMOS, EPISODE 5

In his work with premature babies during the 1970s and '80s, professor
of psychiatry Stephen Porges rediscovered two vagal pathways in the
nervous system that regulate the heart and provide a face-heart connection to communicate what is happening inside our bodies to other people.
These discoveries helped define Polyvagal Theory, and we now have an
easy way to understand and work with our autonomic nervous systems.

The autonomic nervous system could also be called the *automatic*
nervous system since it takes care of our body's basic housekeeping
responsibilities (i.e., breath, heart rate, digestion) without our needing
to pay attention to them. The wonderful thing about this system is
that it not only functions automatically with preprogrammed settings
but, with Polyvagal Theory, it can also be adjusted. To do so, we have
to understand the following three main principles:

1. Autonomic hierarchy: The system is organized around
three building blocks that work in a certain order and
come with preset pathways.

2. Neuroception: The system has a built-in surveillance system that watches for signs of safety and warnings about danger ahead.

3. Co-regulation: Having moments of safely connecting to others is a necessary ingredient for well-being.

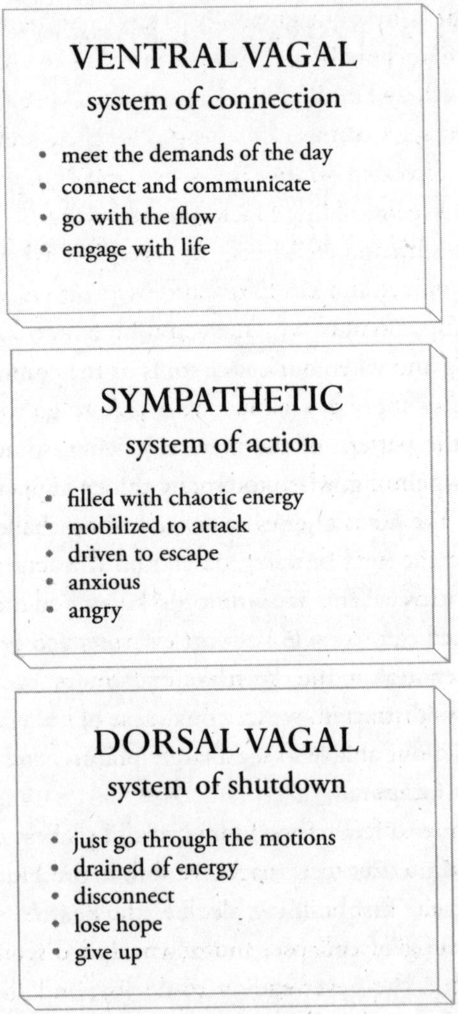

VENTRAL VAGAL
system of connection

- meet the demands of the day
- connect and communicate
- go with the flow
- engage with life

SYMPATHETIC
system of action

- filled with chaotic energy
- mobilized to attack
- driven to escape
- anxious
- angry

DORSAL VAGAL
system of shutdown

- just go through the motions
- drained of energy
- disconnect
- lose hope
- give up

Image 1.1 Three building blocks and emergent qualities

Autonomic Hierarchy:
The Building Blocks of Experience

Through the process of evolution, three building blocks came into being one after the other: dorsal vagal (shutdown) around 500 million years ago, sympathetic (activation) around 400 million years ago, and ventral vagal (connection) around 200 million years ago. This sequential order, called the autonomic hierarchy, is key to understanding how the nervous system anchors in regulation and reacts to challenges in daily living. Each of these building blocks works in a specific way, affecting our biology through connections inside the body and impacting our psychology by directing how we see, sense, and engage with the world.

The ventral vagal building block, the newest of the three, provides a pathway to health and well-being and the place where life feels manageable. We connect and communicate with others, and may join a group or be happy on our own. The common irritations of daily living don't feel so big and when our coffee spills or the commute is too slow, instead of getting angry or anxious, we're able to go with the flow.

Following the pattern of the hierarchy, when something happens that feels overwhelming, when too many things happen all at once, or when it seems like life is a series of never-ending challenges, we move down a step to the next building block and the action taking of the sympathetic pathway. This is commonly known as the place of fight and flight. When our to-do list doesn't ever seem to get smaller, there is never quite enough money to make ends meet, or it feels like our partner is always distracted, we lose our sense of being safe in the present moment and our ability to see a larger picture, and we react either by attacking or escaping.

If we continue to feel trapped in a cycle of endless challenges with no way out and no way to manage, we follow the hierarchy down to the final step to the first building block of the nervous system and the dorsal vagal feeling of collapse, shutdown, and disconnection. Here, the spilled coffee, the never-ending to-do list, and the partner who never seems to be present with us no longer matter. We begin to shut down and disconnect. We may still go through the motions, but with no energy to care. We lose hope that anything will ever change. And because our nervous system follows a predictable sequence, moving from one building block to the next, in order to recover from this place of collapse, we need to find our way to some energy in the sympathetic system and continue on to the regulation of the ventral vagal state.

A good way to get the flavor of each of the three building blocks is by exploring two statements: "The world is . . ." and "I am . . ." Finding the words that describe how you view the world and your place in it brings awareness to the beliefs that are stored in each state. Start in dorsal, the building block at the bottom of the hierarchy, and feel into the experience of disconnection, collapse, and shutdown. Fill in the two sentences "The world is . . ." and "I am . . ." You might find the world is unwelcoming, dark, or empty, and you are untethered, abandoned, or lost. Move up one building block to the overwhelming sympathetic flood of energy and explore the same two sentences. Perhaps the world is chaotic, unmanageable, or terrifying, and, from this place of disorganization and chaos, you are out of control, dysregulated, or in danger. And now move up to the final building block and the state of ventral vagal safety and regulation. From here, how do you fill in the sentences "The world is . . ." and "I am . . ."? You might experience the world as welcoming, beautiful, and inviting of connection and feel okay, alive and well, and filled with possibility. Working in this way with the autonomic hierarchy, we begin to understand the different experiences each autonomic state creates. Reflecting on the two sentences "The world is . . ." and "I am . . . ," we see how dramatically our stories change as we move from one state, one building block, to another.

Neuroception: Your Internal Surveillance System

The second principle of Polyvagal Theory, the internal surveillance system, is defined by the wonderfully descriptive word *neuroception*. Stephen Porges created this word to illustrate how the nervous system (*neuro*) is aware (*ception*) of signs of safety and signals of danger. With a neuroception of safety, we move out into the world and into connection. A neuroception of danger brings a move into sympathetic fight and flight, while a neuroception of life threat takes us into dorsal vagal collapse and shutdown.

Neuroception follows three streams of awareness: inside, outside, and between. Inside listening happens as neuroception attends to what's happening inside your body—your heartbeat, breath rhythms, and muscle action—and inside your organs, especially those involved with your digestion. Outside listening begins in your immediate environment (where you are physically located) and then expands out into the larger world to include neighborhoods, nations, and the global community. The third stream of awareness, listening between, is the way your nervous system communicates with other systems one-on-one or with a group of people. These three streams of embodied listening are always working, micro-moment to micro-moment, below the level of our conscious awareness. Running in the background, neuroception brings about the autonomic state changes that either invite us into connection with people, places, and experiences or move us away from connection and into the protection of fight, flight, or shutdown. Our story, and how we think, feel, and act, begins with neuroception. And while we can't work directly with neuroception, we can work with our body's response to it. When we bring perception to neuroception, we bring an otherwise nonconscious experience into awareness. We can work with our experience by taking the implicit experience of neuroception and explicitly noticing it and turning our attention toward the state that has come alive. As we keep traveling the pathway of awareness, we connect with feelings, beliefs, behaviors, and finally the story that takes us through our days. When we learn to attend to neuroception, we can begin to shape our stories in new ways.

Co-regulation:
Wired for Connection

And finally, the third principle of Polyvagal Theory is the need for finding safe connection with others in the experience of co-regulation. Co-regulation, regulating with another, is an experience that is necessary for survival. We come into the world unable to fend for ourselves and, for the first years of life, we need to be cared for by others. We are physically unable to regulate on our own and naturally turn toward the people around us to meet both our physical and emotional survival needs. As we grow, these experiences of co-regulation offer a foundation to explore regulating on our own.

Even as we learn to self-regulate, the need for co-regulation continues. This is both an essential ingredient for well-being and also a challenge to negotiate. In order to co-regulate, I have to feel safe with you, you have to feel safe with me, and we have to find a way to come into connection and regulate with each other. We turn to a friend to listen or look to a family member for help. We depend on certain people in our lives to show up with a regulated system when we are in need. While the world seems to be increasingly focused on self-regulation and independence, co-regulation is the foundation for safely navigating daily living. We carry the ongoing need to connect with others, and every day we long for and look for opportunities to co-regulate.

> While the world seems to be increasingly focused on self-regulation and independence, co-regulation is the foundation for safely navigating daily living.

It is through these three principles—hierarchy, neuroception, and co-regulation—that we have a way to acknowledge the role biology has in shaping how we move through the world and a guide to engaging with our biology in ways that bring well-being.

Three Elements for Well-Being

The three principles of Polyvagal Theory—building blocks of the hierarchy, internal surveillance through neuroception, and regulating with others—are where we begin to understand and befriend our nervous system. Next we add the elements of well-being—context, choice, and connection—which help the nervous system anchor in safety and regulation. When these three elements are present, we more easily find the way to regulation. When any one of these elements is missing, we feel off balance and experience a sense of unease.

Context comes from the Latin word *contexere*, meaning "to weave together." Through the lens of the nervous system, context involves gathering information about how, what, and why in order to understand, and respond to, experiences. We get cues of safety from explicit communication of the details surrounding an interaction. When contextual information is sent through implicit pathways and not explicitly shared, we often respond in the present moment based on our past experiences. Without explicitly stated information, we are more likely to sense unsafety and move into a pattern of protection. For instance, a friend sends me a message canceling our planned lunch, and without hearing her voice, seeing her face, or having more information, I'm pulled into anxiety and a story that I've done something wrong and my friend is upset with me. When I find out she didn't feel well, the context changes, and instead of feeling abandoned, I feel care and concern.

Choice is the second element necessary for a regulated nervous system. With choice it's possible to be still or move, approach or avoid, connect or protect. When choice is limited or taken away, or when we have a sense of being stuck or trapped without options, we begin to look for a way out. In this search for survival we may feel the mobilizing energy of the sympathetic system with some form of anxiety or anger, or we may feel our energy draining as we are pulled into a dorsal vagal collapse. Even as we move through the simple activities of a day, we are more able to stay anchored in safety and regulation when there are options. On the other end of that experience, when there are unlimited options, we can feel at sea, unable to make a choice. Too many choices can be overwhelming and adhering to a rigid schedule too restrictive. There is a sweet spot for each of us where we have boundaries to create a framework for our choices and routines that include flexibility.

The final element, connection, brings a sense of relationship. The experience of connection encompasses four domains: connection to self, connection to other people (and pets), connection to nature and the world around us, and connection to spirit. With connection we feel safely embodied, accompanied by others, at home in the environment, and in harmony with spirit. When there is a rupture in our sense of connection (losing our sense of self, experiencing a misstep in a relationship, being cut off from nature, or becoming distanced from our experience of spirit), our ability to anchor in safety and regulation is challenged, and we turn to communication and social engagement to try to find our way back into connection. When there is an ongoing disruption of connection, we often reach out in desperation before retreating into despair.

With this beginning look at the organizing principles of Polyvagal Theory and the elements of a regulated system, we can now turn to exploring our autonomic pathways and trying some explorations to engage the nervous system to bring us a sense of well-being.

2

Traveling Autonomic
Pathways

The only journey is the one within.
RAINER MARIA RILKE,
LETTERS TO A YOUNG POET

While we may think our brains are in charge, the heart of our daily experience and the way we navigate the world begins in our bodies with the autonomic nervous system. This is the place where the stories emerge about who we are and how the world works, what we do and how we feel. It is our biology that shapes our experiences of safety and connection.

The story of the autonomic nervous system begins around 500 million years ago with a prehistoric fish called a placoderm and the branch of the parasympathetic system we know as dorsal vagal. To get a sense of this part of the system, think about a turtle moving slowly and steadily through the world. When scared, the turtle immobilizes, disappears into its shell, and waits until it feels safe enough to peek out at the world again. Immobilization and disappearing are the survival strategies of the dorsal vagal system.

Around 400 million years ago, the sympathetic nervous system emerged in another now extinct fish called an acanthodian. With the arrival of the sympathetic nervous system, movement as a survival strategy was added and fight and flight were now possible. To get a flavor of the mobilization of this system imagine a shark attacking or a fish darting to escape.

Finally, around 200 million years ago, the other branch of the parasympathetic nervous system, the ventral vagal system, came into being. The energy of this uniquely mammalian system allows us to feel safe, connect, and communicate. To feel into this system, remember sitting and talking with a friend, think about walking in nature feeling connected to the earth, or if you have a dog or cat, imagine them curled up beside you.

To summarize, our autonomic nervous system is made up of the parasympathetic and sympathetic systems with the vagus providing the primary pathways for the parasympathetic system through the dorsal and ventral branches. All together this gives us access to three pathways, with each pathway bringing its own particular kind of response. (While these terms may still seem hard to remember, it's important to be familiar with them so please bear with me. And remember you'll be naming the three parts of your own nervous system as you continue in this book.)

As each new system emerged, it joined the older system rather than replacing it, and the architecture of the autonomic nervous system became more complex. Now let's move into a deeper exploration of the architecture of this tripartite autonomic nervous system.

Autonomic Nervous System

Sympathetic Nervous System   Parasympathetic Nervous System

Ventral Vagus   Dorsal Vagus

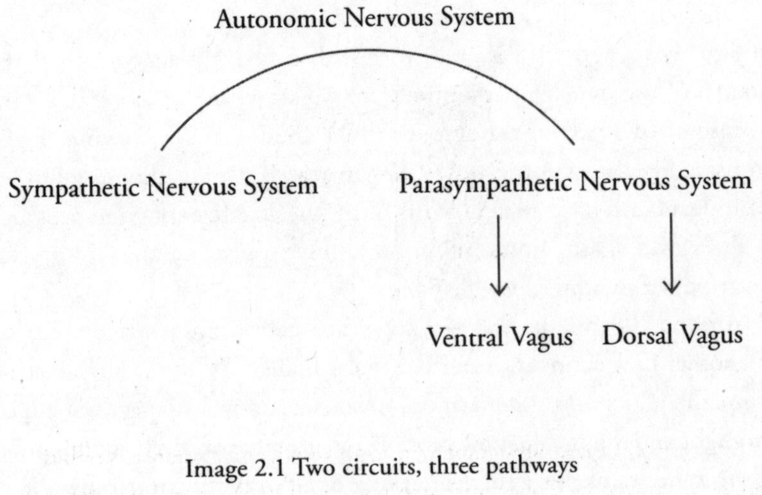

Image 2.1 Two circuits, three pathways

Exploring the Vagal Pathways

The "vagal" in Polyvagal Theory refers to the vagus nerve, which in fact is not a single nerve but rather a bundle of nerves that begins in the brainstem and travels through the body, affecting many different organs along the way. *Vagus* means "wanderer" in Latin, and because of the length of this nerve (the vagus is the longest cranial nerve) and the ways it connects in so many places along its route, it seems it is appropriately named. This photolithograph of a 1543 woodcut by Andreas Vesalius gives us a sense of these intricate pathways.

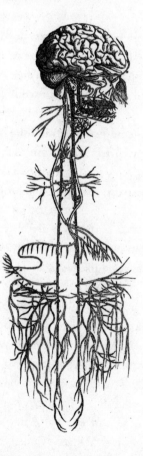

Image 2.2 Photolithograph of a 1543 woodcut by Andreas Vesalius
Credit: Wellcome Collection. Attribution 4.0 International (CC BY 4.0).

Although we will talk about the vagus as one nerve, all twelve of our cranial nerves come in pairs, one on the left side of the brain and one on the right. It is the right vagus nerve that connects to the heart and forms the vagal brake referenced later in this chapter. From the brainstem, the vagus moves down the side of the neck, behind the carotid artery, and around to the front of the body and then travels down through the throat, lungs, and heart to the abdomen and digestive system. To sense into this system with its many branches, put your left hand on the base of your neck and with your right hand trace the pathway of the vagus. Move your right hand around the side of your neck, down your throat to your lungs, your heart, and finally your abdomen. Imagine energy moving up and down this pathway. The information carried along this vagal pathway travels in two directions, with 80 percent of the information going from the body to the brain and 20 percent from the brain to the body. When we are disconnected from our bodies, we are also disconnected from the ability to tune in to the important information being sent from the body to the brain through the vagal pathway.

> When we are disconnected from our bodies, we are also disconnected from the ability to tune in to the important information being sent from the body to the brain through the vagal pathway.

The ventral and dorsal branches of the vagus nerve are identified by the ways they work above or below the diaphragm. The diaphragm is the muscle that separates the chest from the abdomen. If you put one hand on your chest and one just under your ribcage, you are in the vicinity of your diaphragm. From the diaphragm downward is the realm of the dorsal vagus whose everyday, nonreactive responsibility is to regulate healthy digestion. In survival mode, the dorsal vagus takes us out of awareness, out of connection, and into collapse and immobilization. In this survival state, we feel disconnected and numb and have the experience of being here but *not* here and the sense of going through the motions of life without really caring. We suffer with digestive problems as our biological systems move into conservation mode, everything slowing down to maintain just enough energy to keep us alive. We hope that if we disappear, become invisible, and don't feel what's happening or inhabit where we are, we will survive. We escape into not knowing, not feeling, and a sense of not being. As you read this description you may even feel a flavor of your dorsal vagal energy activating in your system.

From the diaphragm upward is the realm of the ventral vagus. This is the place where we anchor in safety and can both self- and co-regulate. Our heart rate is regulated, and our breath is natural and full. We take pleasure in seeing the faces of friends and are able to tune in to conversations and tune out distractions. In a ventral vagal state we can acknowledge distress, explore options, and reach out for and offer support. We are resourced and resourceful. Our attention is focused on connection to ourselves, to others, to the world, and to spirit. This is a place of well-being. As you read this description, see if you can sense this energy and feel your ventral vagal state come alive.

With a beginning awareness of the vagal system, take a moment and move between the two vagal pathways. Place one hand on the base of your skull and the other hand over your heart. Imagine the ventral vagal pathway and feel the energy moving between your two hands. Take a moment to acknowledge the abilities for regulation and connection this system brings. And now move your hand from your heart to your abdomen. With one hand on your brainstem and one hand on your abdomen you're connected to the dorsal vagal pathway. Imagine this pathway and feel the energy that moves here. Take a moment and acknowledge the ways this system works on your behalf, both nourishing you through your digestive processes and protecting you when necessary by taking you out of awareness.

The Vagal Brake

One important ventral vagal circuit is the vagal brake. This particular circuit leaves the brainstem and connects with the sinoatrial node of the heart—the heart's pacemaker—and it is through this connection that our heart rhythms are regulated. The vagal brake slows the heart rate to a healthy number of beats per minute (between sixty and eighty). Without this regulating influence, the heart would beat dangerously fast. Because of the ways this pathway regulates heart rate, it is called the vagal brake. Like all efficient braking mechanisms, the vagal brake works to both slow down and speed up heart rate and bring the right degree of energy needed to successfully navigate moment to moment.

The vagal brake also regulates our respiratory rhythm. It moves in a subtle pattern of release and reengagement with every breath cycle. On each inhalation the vagal brake offers a slight release and the heart rate speeds up just a bit, and then on the exhalation the vagal brake reengages, and the heart rate returns to a slower beat. To get a sense of how the vagal brake works, think about the hand brakes on a bicycle. When you're riding downhill and want to go faster, you gently release the brakes and the wheels spin more quickly. Then, when you want to slow down, you gently squeeze the brakes. The vagal pathway to your heart doesn't actually physically release and reconnect like the brakes on a bicycle; instead it becomes more active and less active through the use of electrical signals and neurotransmitters.

The function of the vagal brake is to allow us to feel, and use, some of the mobilizing energy of the sympathetic nervous system without being pulled into the survival state of fight and flight. As the vagal brake releases a bit, the energy in the sympathetic system is felt more strongly, mobilizing the system. And then, as the vagal brake reengages, there is a return to feeling less of the mobilizing energy of the sympathetic system.

Exploration:
Using Your Vagal Brake

This exploration can be done either seated or standing. Start by imagining you have one foot in ventral vagal regulation and your other foot in sympathetic mobilization. (You can place one foot in front of the other or your feet can be side by side.) Keep both feet on the ground and begin to shift your weight between your feet, rocking slightly from one to the other. Follow your breath cycle. Inhale and rock toward the foot in sympathetic, then exhale and shift your weight back to the foot in ventral. Move through several breath cycles and get a sense of the rhythm of your vagal brake releasing and reengaging.

As the vagal brake begins to release, we have access to a range of responses, including feeling engaged, joyful, excited, passionate, playful, attentive, alert, and watchful all while still under the regulation of the ventral vagal system. Without the vagal brake we lose our anchor in safety and connection and move into the protective states of fight and flight. Experiment with finding the edges of release. Shift your weight so that you are almost fully tipped into sympathetic mobilization. Feel what happens as you begin to lose your balance. And then bring yourself back to feeling the solid ground under the foot that's anchored in ventral.

Now shift in the direction of having your weight fully on the foot that's anchored in ventral while the foot in sympathetic just lightly touches the ground. Feel what happens here. Experiment with the ways your vagal brake allows you to mobilize energy and then helps you return to calm. Feel how the vagal brake holds the boundary between ventral safety and regulation and a sympathetic survival response.

Now that you have a sense of your vagal brake, you can begin to play with shifting the balance between energy and calm. Practice staying anchored in safety and feeling mobilized. Move between rest and action. Explore the full range of experiences that emerge as you release and reengage your vagal brake.

Imagine commonly occurring experiences in which you need to either be energized or calm and use your vagal brake to successfully meet the moment. Bring to mind a moment when you need more energy and release your brake to meet that need. Then bring to mind a moment when you are wanting to feel more at ease and reengage your brake. You can remember moments and play with releasing and reengaging your vagal brake to imagine how the right amount of energy might have changed the experience. Once you gain confidence in your ability to stay anchored, you can intentionally adjust the balance toward calm when you feel a rise in anxiety or toward more energy when you need to take action.

The Energy of the Sympathetic System

The sympathetic system is a spinal nerve system that emerges from the thoracic and lumbar regions in the middle part of the back. To get a sense of this, reach one hand gently down from your neck and reach your other hand gently up from your waist. The space between your hands is roughly where your sympathetic nervous system is located. The energy of the sympathetic nervous system is vital to our ability to move through the world. It has a regulating role in pumping blood and managing heart rhythms and breath patterns. As you discovered with the vagal brake exploration, the energies of the ventral and sympathetic systems can work in cooperation, enlivening our experience. But if we lose connection to the vagal brake, we lose our anchor in the ventral system and move out of safety into a state of sympathetic survival. When enlisted in a survival mode, the sympathetic system activates fight and flight, and the hypothalamic-pituitary-adrenal (HPA) axis (a circuit that connects the hypothalamus and pituitary gland in your brain with the adrenals that sit on top of your kidneys) begins to release cortisol and adrenaline.

A car suddenly pulling out in front of you on the highway, your child reaching toward a hot stove, or your dog running for the road are the kinds of experiences that bring a quick burst of adrenaline. We experience an immediate response to manage the event and then return to regulation when it's over. Take a moment and think about a time when you had that quick jolt of adrenaline. Your body probably holds the memory and will bring it alive as you remember.

In addition to this quick, short-term adrenaline-fueled response, the sympathetic system also responds to distress with the release of cortisol.

Persistent experiences like being surrounded by difficult people, living in a place that feels unsafe, or working in an environment that feels toxic can bring an ongoing cortisol response that feels like a swirl of energy and leaves you in an unending, and unattainable, search for calm.

Think about your daily life. Do you have a list of endless demands? Do you feel like you have responsibilities that keep adding up no matter what you do? Notice your body's response to this sympathetically fueled state.

In our evolutionary history, being a part of a tribe was essential for survival. We survived in groups. There was strength in numbers. When we are anchored in the safety of ventral regulation, we look for connection and see possibilities for friendship. Moving out of ventral safety into the energy of the sympathetic system, we have a sense of impending danger and enter into fight and flight. The world feels like an unsafe place filled with unsafe people. In this state we misread cues and experience neutral faces and certain tones of voice as signs of danger. Our hearing is tuned to listen for sounds of danger, and it's easy to miss the sounds of friendly voices around us. We scan the environment, no longer just aware and alert; we are now alarmed and hypervigilant. We are on our own, separated from others, and we look at the world from an "us vs. them" or "me vs. you" mindset.

Moving Between States

Knowing how each pathway works individually, we can now look at how states work together and explore the relationship between them. Over the course of evolution, the three pathways of the autonomic nervous system (dorsal, sympathetic, and ventral) emerged and formed the building blocks of the system (hierarchy). Our preferred place, the place where we find experiences of health, growth, and restoration, is anchored in the ventral vagal state of safety and connection. When we are pulled out of regulation, the first move is into the sympathetic system of mobilization and protection through action taking. The final step takes us to the dorsal vagal system of immobilization and protection through disconnection. This predictable order of moving between autonomic states means we can track our journey into dysregulation and have a roadmap to find our way back to the safety of regulation.

We naturally travel between states, routinely moving out of ventral regulation into sympathetic or dorsal dysregulation and back again. Leaving regulation isn't the problem. In fact, the goal is not to stay in a state of regulation but rather to know where we are, recognize when we're moving out of regulation and being pulled into a survival response, and be able to return to regulation. The ability to flexibly move between states is a sign of well-being and resilience. It is when we are caught in dysregulation, unable to find our way back to regulation, that we feel distress. When we get pulled out of ventral safety and connection and get lost in a place of dysregulation, we move from flexibility to rigidity and feel the effects of a nervous system that is stuck in the intensity of sympathetic mobilization or dorsal shutdown.

> The ability to flexibly move between states is a sign of well-being and resilience. It is when we are caught in dysregulation, unable to find our way back to regulation, that we feel distress.

When anchored in the regulating energy of the ventral vagal state, the autonomic nervous system is in balance and we experience the sense of well-being that comes with a feeling of healthy homeostasis. In times of challenge, we are able to reflect (rather than react), collaborate, and communicate. Stop for a moment and think about a time when you felt regulated and solved a problem on your own or found a solution with someone else. If we're not successful in meeting and managing the challenge here, we move out of regulation into sympathetic mobilization and the energy of fight and flight. Pause here and remember a time when you experienced that intensely activating energy and were driven to stay and argue or felt desperate to get away. Finally, if taking action doesn't resolve the challenge and we feel trapped, we move to dorsal vagal shutdown. Think about a time when you felt a flavor of giving up or going along without really being present or caring.

Because of the way the nervous system was formed, one building block on top of the other, in order to return to safety and regulation from the state of collapse, we have to travel through sympathetic mobilization without getting caught in a fight-or-flight response. A moment of safe mobilization can take many forms. It might start with a small body movement, a shared look with someone, or even a thought that feels like the beginning of a possibility. The essential element of this moment of mobilization is a return of energy that is not so big or intense that it becomes a cue of danger but rather is felt as a cue of safety that shows the way back to regulation. From this safe starting point we can continue to feel energy returning and find our way back to ventral regulation.

It's a normal human experience to move through states in both small shifts and bigger ways many times a day. Consider the states you have already visited today in moments of ease, small moments that were slightly charged, others that felt empty, or even more intense moments of fight, flight, or collapse. Remember, the common experience of moving in and out of states is not a barrier to well-being. It's only when we move out of safety and connection into one of the adaptive survival responses and can't find our way back to a state of regulation that we suffer physically and psychologically. Ventral vagal energy is the active ingredient in safety and connection. Without this regulating influence, we suffer physical, emotional, relational, and spiritual distress. But when our ventral vagal state is active and in charge, the sympathetic and dorsal vagal systems work in the background and all three states work together, creating physical and psychological well-being.

Exploration:
Befriending the Autonomic Hierarchy

With an understanding of the architecture, responsibilities, and survival actions of each autonomic state, we can move from cognition to embodied awareness. Our starting point is in the state of healthy homeostasis. Here the ventral vagal energy is overseeing the entire system, bringing regulation to allow the sympathetic and dorsal systems to work in the background.

I often imagine my ventral vagal state surrounding the sympathetic and dorsal systems, holding them in a warm embrace. The image I have been using recently for the ventral vagal state is a colorful umbrella that is sheltering the sympathetic and dorsal vagal states, keeping them safe and dry. What image comes to mind for you? How does this come alive in your body? How does your energy flow when your three states are connected and communicating? Take a moment to find your image and notice this embodied sense of well-being.

Next explore what happens in your body when your sympathetic and dorsal states act on their own. Begin with the dorsal vagal state. What changes as you move from regulation to disconnection? Where does your body hold the feeling of collapse or shutdown? Move up into sympathetic mobilization. Let your nervous system show you the places in your body where you feel this state come alive.

And now find a name for each of the three states. While you may ultimately choose to stick with the biological terms *ventral, sympathetic,* and *dorsal,* experiment with naming your states with your own labels. Turn inward, connect with each state again, and see what names you hear (e.g., *sunny, stormy, foggy; flow, chaos, collapse; connected, activated, gone*). Write down combinations of names that catch your interest and play with them until you find three that fit together and represent your experience.

When we view a landscape, we see the ways it has been shaped both by human actions and natural events. We can explore our autonomic states through the imagery of landscapes. Each autonomic state has its own landscape. There are landscapes for our everyday, nonreactive states, our survival states, and our state of safety and connection. In the following explorations, you're invited to use a journal to document your autonomic landscapes. Remember you can document in written form with single words, bullet points, or a longer piece of writing, or you might choose some form of art (i.e., drawing, photography, collage).

Exploration:
Regulated Landscapes

Begin by venturing into the world of ventral regulation. To find your way there, remember the name you gave this state and go to the place in your body where you feel the flow of regulating energy. Connect with a memory of a time when you felt a moment, or even a micro-moment, of safety and connection. Experiment until you find your way to anchor in regulation. When you arrive, look around. You might see an actual environment, elements of the natural world, or a home. You might see colors or feel energy. In this place of regulation that brings possibilities and invites exploration, take some time to document what you find here.

Next we can explore the everyday experiences of the dorsal and sympathetic systems; not their survival roles but their daily actions that support health and well-being. Start with the slow and steady beat of your dorsal vagal system. What is the landscape here? What images, colors, words, and sense of energy live here? Document in your journal the features of the landscape in this safe, everyday dorsal experience that brings nutrients to nourish you and is necessary for well-being.

Now, move to the landscape of your sympathetic system, not as it activates in fight and flight but in the safe, mobilizing energy that supports heart and breath rhythms, regulates temperature, and brings movement. What is it like here? What images, colors, and words appear? Notice the ways energy and movement are similar to or different from the dorsal landscape. Document what you find.

End by returning to where you began in the safety and regulation of a ventral vagal state and reflect on the three landscapes of your regulated nervous system.

Exploration:
Survival Landscapes

With awareness of the regulated, nonreactive landscapes, our next exploration is a look at the survival landscapes. In order to get to know these places without getting pulled into them, we want to travel to the other states while keeping an anchor in the ventral landscape. My ventral vagal landscape is by the sea, and I imagine taking a small beach stone with me to remind me that I'm safely anchored there. Look for something in your ventral landscape that you can take with you.

With the reminder of your anchor in safety and regulation, make the trip to your dorsal state and see the survival landscape. Dip into a moment when you felt disconnected from the world and a flavor of hopelessness entered into your thoughts. Notice the ways it is different from the nonreactive, everyday landscape. The survival landscape offers protection through disconnection and collapse. If you begin to feel pulled into shutdown, bring your attention to what you brought with you from your ventral landscape and remember you are still connected to the safety and regulation of that place. Use your journal to document the features of your dorsal vagal landscape.

The next step is into the sympathetic survival state where there's too much energy; it's a bit disorganized, a bit chaotic, and you feel the flavor of fight and flight. Bring to mind a time when you were pulled into anxiety or anger and take just a small step into that state. When you look around, what do you see? Remember, you brought a piece of your ventral vagal landscape with you to keep you from getting lost here and hijacked by the sympathetic survival energy. Document in your journal what you find here.

To end this exercise, come back to where you began in the landscape of ventral vagal safety and connection. Rest here for a moment and take time to reflect on what you discovered in your two survival landscapes.

The autonomic nervous system brings immobilizing, activating, and regulating actions. We have an inherent longing to be in the regulation of the ventral vagal system and an embodied wisdom on how to get there. The pathway back to connection from fight, flight, or collapse is there in all of us. It may be obscured or not well traveled due to our personal life experiences, but our biology knows the way, and we can find our way home.

3

Learning to Listen

To me, the body says what words cannot.
MARTHA GRAHAM,
NEW YORK TIMES INTERVIEW, 1985

Listening is an essential part of befriending your autonomic nervous system and, in the beginning, it can feel very odd to tune in and listen. After all, this is an automatic system that works without the need for us to pay attention. With the act of listening and attending to what is happening in our bodies, we gain some management over our system and more regulation in our lives. When we learn to listen, we create the ability to reflect and not simply react. As we learn to partner with our nervous system, we begin to experience well-being.

Partnering with the nervous system is a two-step process. First, we need to have an understanding of how the system works, and second, we need to use that information to create a life of well-being. I'm often asked if, when we create a relationship with our nervous system, we discover that everything we feel and think and do is simply an outcome of our biology. For me, the answer to that question is no. Understanding how our autonomic nervous system works may take away the mystery of how we move through the world, but it also invites the magic of our human experience. When we understand how our biology creates the platform for our experiences and how our autonomic state sets the landscape for our stories, we can embrace the many magical moments that make life such an extraordinary, miraculous experience.

A polyvagal-informed understanding of our feelings, thoughts, and behaviors offers a way to be with our experiences instead of being hijacked by them. When we're flooded by our emotions, we lose connection to regulation and lose the ability for reflection. From an anchor in ventral safety and regulation, we can connect to our states and listen to our stories with the distance needed for reflection. When we learn to listen to our nervous system, we create skills to turn toward our experiences with curiosity and regain the ability to respond rather than simply react.

Autonomic listening is inextricably linked with the need for self-compassion. Self-compassion is an emergent property of the ventral vagal system. Survival states automatically activate self-criticism, so when we move out of safety and connection into a state of protection, we lose the capacity for self-compassion. With the ability to recognize a moment of distress and notice the autonomic state, we move into a moment of awareness instead of simply being swept deeper into dysregulation.

Kristin Neff and Chris Germer have developed a lovely, simple compassion practice to use when we feel a moment of distress. To try this practice, designed to help us move from self-criticism to self-compassion, bring up a moment when you felt distress and read these three phrases[1]:

1. This is a moment of suffering.

2. Suffering is a part of life.

3. May I be kind to myself.

If it feels soothing, you can place a hand on your heart and repeat these phrases.

Exploration:
The Language of the Nervous System

Now, let's take the essence of the three phrases and rewrite them looking through the lens of the nervous system. My phrases sound like this:

1. My nervous system is in a survival response.

2. Moments of protection happen for everyone.

3. May I bring some ventral vagal energy to this moment.

The first statement is a recognition that you have entered a state of dysregulation. Find the words that describe your move out of connection into protection. The second statement recognizes the universal experience of dysregulation. What words convey that for you? And the third statement invites a moment, or a micro-moment, of ventral vagal reconnection. How would you say that?

Now, with your three phrases, bring to mind a moment of distress, either a moment of beginning to feel the energy of fight and flight or the pull out of connection into collapse. Let some of that survival energy into your system and say your three phrases to yourself. Do your phrases help you begin to find your way back to regulation where you have access to self-compassion? Rewrite your phrases if needed until you find the words that help you connect with self-compassion.

By noticing a moment, or a micro-moment, of autonomic dysregulation and bringing some self-compassion to it, we enter into a process of listening. The journalist and writing teacher Brenda Ueland once described listening as a "magnetic and strange thing, a creative force."[2] Listening to the autonomic nervous system is just that kind of experience. Once we begin, there's a powerful pull to continue and see where the listening will lead. While listening to the nervous system is an unfamiliar experience to be sure, when we are anchored in ventral regulation, we experience what is unfamiliar as interesting rather than as a cue of danger. Autonomic listening leads to an invitation to be creative in finding shaping practices that are just right for our nervous system.

Engaging in moments of befriending and learning to listen change the way we see our own experiences and the way we see the world. Our biology shapes each moment and informs how we navigate the world. We begin to understand ourselves and others in a new way when we understand patterns of autonomic responding.

Much of the time we are carried on a stream of autonomic state shifts without conscious awareness. The nervous system reliably does its job in the background, increasing and decreasing energy to meet the needs of the moment. Stop for a moment and listen in. Place a hand over your heart and connect to your heartbeat. Find your breath with a hand on your chest, abdomen, side ribs, or small of your back or under your nostrils. Tune in to these autonomically guided rhythms. Take a moment and attend to each beat, each inhale and exhale. Feel how much energy and attention it takes. If we actually had to think about these autonomic functions, all of our attention would be focused on our biology. The automaticity of the autonomic nervous system makes it possible for us to attend to other things; to create, to imagine, and to connect with others in the world.

> Engaging in moments of befriending and learning to listen change the way we see our own experiences and the way we see the world.

While the autonomic nervous system works without the need for us to listen in and watch over it, learning to tune in to autonomic states is an important skill. We often have a thought or a feeling and take action without knowing what led us to those responses. Bring to mind a time when you held a belief without knowing where it came from. Maybe you found yourself thinking "I'm a failure" or "I'm a misfit" or "I'm so blessed." Think about a time when you were caught in a feeling without understanding why. You might remember feeling sad even though you were in a group of happy people or waking up one morning with a feeling of excitement even though it was just an ordinary day. Look for a feeling that was unexpected. Finally, remember a time when you acted in a certain way without knowing why. Maybe you found yourself having an intense response to a situation that didn't make sense, or you were pulled into action without even thinking about it.

We depend on our autonomic nervous system to guide us and protect us. We want our biology to regulate our breath and heart rhythms, activate energy and reinstate calm, and bring a thought, a feeling, or a behavior that takes us toward or away from people, places, and experiences in just the right way for the present moment. We also want to be able to intentionally tune in and listen. Listening is an act of autonomic awareness and an essential ingredient in learning to regulate our systems. With awareness comes understanding and with understanding comes choice.

The *Merriam-Webster* online dictionary defines listening as "hearing something with thoughtful attention."[3] As we learn to listen to our autonomic responses and hear where our system has taken us, we also need to bring the essential ingredient of thoughtful attention. When we come into awareness, we often feel judgment and self-criticism. We move into meaning making, forgetting that our biology is not assigning motivation or making moral meaning but simply responding. Instead of attributing intention to our autonomic actions, we need to remember that our behaviors, feelings, and beliefs are emerging from an autonomic state, and our autonomic nervous system is working in service of our survival.

The challenge is to learn to tune in and turn toward your nervous system, bring curiosity and compassion to the experience, and stay out of judgment and self-criticism as you explore where your autonomic nervous system takes you. Some of the phrases I use to tune in and turn toward are as follows:

"It's my biology wanting to send me a message."

"My job is just to listen."

"I can tune in, turn toward, and listen without needing to make meaning."

What can you say to yourself to bring curiosity and self-compassion to the process of listening? You'll know when you find the phrase that fits when your autonomic nervous system says yes—not when your brain says yes, but when your biology says yes. The autonomic nervous system has an important role in our experiences of approaching, avoiding, and feeling ambivalent. Each autonomic state plays a part in how we say yes, no, and maybe. Knowing the many different ways these experiences emerge and being able to identify which state is sending the message are essential skills.

Exploration:
The Autonomic Experiences
of Yes, No, and Maybe

Start by exploring the different qualities of saying no. How do you say no when driven by your sympathetic system and the mobilized energy that comes from fight and flight? What are the qualities of saying no when you are in a dorsal collapse, not caring what happens? And what is the experience when you are anchored in ventral regulation and setting a boundary from a state of safety?

Now think of something you're unsure about. How does your autonomic nervous system show you an ambivalent response? Experiment with the ways each of your states sends you a message. Explore the ways you say maybe when you are charged with too much energy, fueled by fear or anxiety and not able to make a decision. Feel the flavor of saying maybe that emerges when your energy drains away and you are feeling hopeless, unable to even process the question. Find the regulated experience of ambivalence where you feel safe and able to say maybe in a way that opens the door to possibilities.

Finally move to something that's a yes for you. How does your autonomic nervous system show you that? What does saying yes sound like and feel like when someone makes a demand and you feel you have no other choice but to agree? What happens when you say yes from a place of despair where you don't have the energy to care what happens? And how do you say yes when you are in a regulated state of safety and feel like you have a choice about your response? Practice saying yes from an anchor in ventral regulation where you are willing to engage and interested in moving forward.

Exploration:
Anchoring in Curiosity

With this new way of knowing how your system sends you information about no, maybe, and yes, the next step is to turn your attention to finding a phrase that helps you say a regulated yes and stay anchored in the state of listening with curiosity. A phrase I use is "I'm ready to see what's possible." Play with words until you find ones that support you in saying yes to exploring the process of tuning in and listening to your nervous system. Use your phrase to anchor in curiosity and stay out of judgment as we explore a new way of listening.

Bring your attention to where you are in this moment. What state are you inhabiting right now? You might think back to chapter 2 when you first explored the qualities of the ventral, sympathetic, and dorsal states: the ventral feelings of being safe, connected, organized, and resourced; the sympathetic flood of mobilizing energy that takes you out of connection into fight and flight; the dorsal place of collapsing, numbing, and disappearing. Use those markers to identify where you are right now. What state is alive? You can use the phrase you created to help anchor in curiosity so you can safely travel inward and notice the state.

As you begin to get comfortable with this way of listening, expand the practice from the present moment to the recent past. Start by thinking about the past five minutes and where your autonomic nervous system took you. What states did you visit? The focus is to simply tune in and listen without being pulled into meaning making. With practice, you might decide to expand your reflection to fifteen minutes or longer. As you gain skill in this way of reflecting, you might want to stop during the day and listen periodically or make time to reflect at the end of the day. There's no one way to practice; rather the work is defined by the time that your nervous system says yes to.

However you listen, this exploration is a way to connect and bring awareness to the autonomic states that you experience as you move through the day.

This is the foundation of learning to listen. As you tune in and bring awareness to your states, begin to explore some of these questions: Are these familiar places? Have you found a state that you don't visit very often? Do you see a pattern that you know well or is there an interesting new pattern emerging? Remember, this is an information-gathering experience, not a meaning-making one. Take time to reflect and document what you're learning in your journal.

Exploration: Outside In and Inside Out

Having completed this beginning exploration of how to listen with self-compassion and curiosity, we can now think about two different ways to listen: from the outside in and the inside out. For many of us, in the beginning, it is easier to start with listening from the outside in. You can use the following questions to begin to listen from the outside in:

Where am I? (Locate yourself in time and space.)

What's happening in the environment?

Who is around?

What am I doing?

What state has been activated?

Notice that the questions are designed to evoke curiosity, identify concrete external experiences, and lead you to identifying your autonomic state. Use these five questions to practice listening from the outside in.

Listening from the inside out is an equally important way to connect. And just like with listening from the outside in, the goal as you explore this way of listening is to stay in curiosity and out of meaning making.

What am I sensing in my body?

Where is energy moving?

Where is energy not moving?

Do I feel filled?

Do I feel empty?

What state is active in this moment?

Similar to the first list, these questions are also designed to evoke curiosity, this time by bringing attention to internal experiences to support connection with your autonomic state.

To end this chapter, let's listen one more time to the messages from your nervous system. Imagine you're an autonomic explorer learning about your system. Pause for just a moment. Step out of the stream of activity that surrounds you and move into connection with your inner world of autonomic activity. You might metaphorically take that step into inner connection, or you might want to physically step out of the flow of the world around you and into a space that brings the quiet you need to turn inward and listen. Leave behind any need to make meaning and come to the place where you can simply be curious about the workings of your autonomic nervous system.

Settle into that place for just a moment. Remember, you're just listening with thoughtful attention. What autonomic energies do you sense stirring? What is the message your nervous system is sending? Tune in and turn toward those messages with curiosity and listen without judgment. When you have heard what your nervous system wants you to know, come back into the present moment and outward awareness. Bring the sense of connection with your autonomic nervous system with you. Remember, this inner connection is always available to you. Make an intention to continue to tune in and listen.

The nervous system speaks in its own language and in order to listen, we need to understand that language. Becoming fluent in a new language takes time and practice. When we enter into the conversation with curiosity, we begin to connect with the energy that is just beneath the surface of awareness and hear the autonomic stories that are shaping our days.

4

The Longing for
Connection

I am human because I belong to the whole, to the
community, to the nation, to the tribe, to the earth.

ARCHBISHOP DESMOND TUTU,
FOREWORD TO *DIGNITY*

We come into the world wired for connection. With our first breath we embark on a lifelong quest to feel safe in our bodies, in our environments, and in our relationships with others. As my colleague Stephen Porges has often expressed to me, our longing is not simply to feel safe but to feel safe in the arms of another. Co-regulation is what is called a biological imperative, meaning we don't survive without it. We are born needing to be welcomed by another human being and this essential need lasts for a lifetime. Evolutionary biologist Theodosius Dobzhansky spoke to this in his book *Mankind Evolving*, when he wrote "the fittest may also be the gentlest, because survival often requires mutual help and cooperation."[1]

The stories of children living in orphanages or growing up in homes without predictably safe adults illustrate what happens when basic survival needs are met but there is no safe and predictable sense of connection to another person. Without those connections we have more difficulty regulating emotions, experience low self-esteem, and struggle to create lasting, healthy relationships. While we may give up the active search for people to connect with, our nervous system never stops looking for, waiting for, and longing for connection. Until the day we die, we long for safe and reliable connections. Co-regulation is essential; first for survival and then for living a life of well-being.

To meet our needs for connection, it's not necessary to have relationships that are always in balance. Rather, we require relationships that are reciprocal. In fact, we build resilience in relationships when we feel connected, experience a rupture, and find our way back to repair. It's only when ruptures happen without repair that our longing for connection brings suffering. The cycle of reciprocity, rupture, and repair is the nature of healthy relationships.[2]

> Until the day we die, we long for safe and reliable connections. Co-regulation is essential; first for survival and then for living a life of well-being.

We are wired for connection, wish for connection, and wait for connection, and yet so often it's been in our connections that we have felt not seen, not understood, not welcomed, and not safe. Sebern Fisher, a leading expert on neurofeedback, offers that when we miss experiences of being with people with whom we can safely and predictably co-regulate, what she calls an "organizing other," our nervous system is stunned.[3] At an embodied level, we are nourished in moments of connection with people who are regulated, safe, and welcoming and shocked when we don't have enough of those experiences.

The lack of connection brings health consequences and creates a daily experience of suffering. The research on the consequences of being out of connection shows that when we are lonely, we are at a higher risk for physical disease and psychological dis-ease. Our immune function is impacted, and we have higher levels of inflammation and a higher risk for cancer, heart disease, and diabetes. We suffer with ongoing anxiety or depression, and as we age these risks increase.[4] Interestingly, the research shows that it is not our actual circumstances but rather a perception of being lonely that creates the risk.[5] We can be surrounded by people and feel connected or be surrounded by people and feel profoundly alone.

Think about a time when you were with people and felt disconnected and a time when you were with people and felt connected.

Both are common experiences. The first takes you either to sympathetic fight and flight or dorsal shutdown and collapse, and the second helps you feel anchored in ventral safety and connection.

The Social Engagement System

Our biology has evolved to include a system known as the social engagement system. When the ventral vagal building block was added, five circuits came into connection in the brainstem and the human social engagement system came to life. The ventral vagal pathway to the heart, joined with the nerves that control our eyes, ears, voice, and the way we move our head, make the social engagement system truly a biological face-heart connection.

To locate your social engagement system, start by placing your hands at the base of your skull where your brainstem meets your spinal cord. This is the hub of the social engagement system. Now place one hand on the side of your face and the other hand over your heart. Imagine energy moving between your hands, traveling from your face to your heart and your heart to your face. Follow this pathway in both directions. It is through this face-heart connection that we listen for sounds of welcome, look for friendly faces, and turn and tilt our heads in search of safety. Micro-moment to micro-moment, through our eyes, ears, voice, and head movements, our social engagement system broadcasts an invitation for connection with someone or sends them a warning to keep their distance. In addition to sending signals of welcome or warning, our social engagement system looks for signs from others to let us know it's safe to come into connection.

Exploration: Elements of the Social Engagement System

Signals from the Eyes

We can explore the elements of the social engagement system one at a time starting with the eyes. Around our eyes is a muscle called the orbicularis oculi. This muscle opens and closes the eyelid and contributes to our crow's feet, the wrinkles around our eyes that are part of our autonomic story. The upper third of the face is where the autonomic nervous system looks first to see if someone is a friend or a foe.

Our eyes commonly shift many times a day, sometimes sending a stare or glare, other moments moving into a neutral look, and still other times offering a warm, inviting gaze. Let's experiment with these three ways of looking. Start with a stare by sending a strong, focused look with a hint of a glare. You might feel your eyes reaching out from their sockets as you send a message with a clear agenda. Now shift to a more neutral way of looking. This is a less strongly focused action where you might feel your eyes settling back into their sockets a bit. This way of looking doesn't carry a lot of information and can be confusing to another person as they attempt to assess danger and safety. Finally, end with a gaze. Send a soft, warm look. Feel your eyes resting easily in their sockets as you extend an invitation for connection and send signals of safety. We naturally move through these nuanced ways of looking many times a day. Without the important element of context (see chapter 1), we move toward or away from connection depending on how the look we receive is filtered through our own past experiences.

Sounds of Safety and Danger

The ears are another important part of the social engagement system. When we're feeling safe and regulated, our hearing is tuned to the frequency of the human voice, and we listen for sounds of friendship. When we begin to feel anxious or uneasy, we listen for sounds of danger and the presence of predators in order to stay safe. Low-frequency sounds commonly bring either a flight or collapse response while high-frequency sounds draw our attention as we look to find the source of what is wrong. You can explore your autonomic response to sound by listening to different sounds and noticing if you are pulled toward connection with a desire to come closer or want to move away and disconnect.

The environment around us is filled with sound, creating what is known as a soundscape.[6] Take some time and begin to tune in to your soundscape. What are the sounds around you? As you listen, let your awareness move beneath the first layer of sound and tune in to the variety of sounds that make up your soundscape. Begin to notice the soundscapes that surround you as you move through your day and the ways your nervous system responds. The soundscape I find by the sea is where I feel welcomed. Where are the soundscapes that invite you in?

Our soundscapes are filled with particular sounds called soundmarks.[7] Some soundmarks help us anchor in regulation while others prompt a move into mobilization or shutdown. For me, waves and the sound of the ocean anchor me in ventral while for others the same soundmarks can activate a move into sympathetic fight and flight or dorsal shutdown. Tune in to the soundmarks in the different environments you encounter. Which ones welcome you and which ones send a warning? Imagine a soundscape that helps you anchor in ventral and notice the soundmarks that are important to you. When we can identify soundmarks that help us anchor in safety and regulation, we can begin to shape our soundscapes to be autonomically nourishing.

The word *prosody* is used to describe the inflection and rhythm of a voice. Prosody can be thought of as the music of our voice. Through our tone and the rise and fall of our voice as we speak, we transmit our underlying intention. The nervous system listens to this intonation before it takes in any information. When we hear a tone that welcomes, we tune in to the conversation, and when we hear a tone of warning, we pay attention to cues of danger and miss the meaning of the words. We listen to the sounds of words before we look for the meanings of those words.

In addition to words, we often communicate through nonlanguage sounds called vocal bursts. These are sounds like "mmm," "huh," and "uh oh" that we commonly use in everyday conversations. Vocal bursts are universally understood sounds. They are recognized across cultures and even across species (we use these sounds when we talk to our pets). We communicate clearly without needing words. It's reassuring to remember that when words are hard to find and when we don't know quite what to say, we can use a vocal burst and reliably transmit our intentions to another person.[8]

Messages from Head Movements

Finally, we can look at the ways we tilt and turn our heads. There is a natural movement to the head, a slight turn and a tilt that is a sign of safety. You can get a sense of this by noticing what happens when you talk while keeping your head straight and unmoving and comparing that to what happens when you talk and let your head move in a way that feels natural. While this may seem like a simple, unimportant movement, in fact, when we turn and tilt our heads, we are sending meaningful signals of safety.

Pathways of Connection

We're nourished by the essential connections to self, to others, to the world, and to spirit. These connections are grounded in the nervous system. When we are anchored in ventral safety and regulation, we are ready for connection. When we lose our anchor in ventral, we also lose our capacity for connection. Each of the four connections (self, other, world, spirit) is important for well-being. We have our own individual needs around the combination of connections that helps us feel nourished and our own individual ways of utilizing each pathway. Rather than an equation we solve once, the ratios are always changing. Our work is to tune in and know what's needed today, this week, or even in this moment. We need to listen not to the stories that our brain tells us about what we need or what the people around us think we need but to what our nervous system is asking for. When we are anchored in ventral safety and regulation, we can bring curiosity to the combination of connections that nurture and sustain us.

Exploration:
Four Connections

Connection with Self

What happens when we turn to connect inward? Rumi in his poem "The Guest House" wrote, "This being human is a guest house," and Walt Whitman in his poem "Song of Myself, 51" wrote, "I am large, I contain multitudes." The Internal Family Systems (IFS) model developed by Richard Schwartz reminds us that we are all a normal multiplicity. We are an integrated system, both one and many. We all have parts.

In fact, it is a common occurrence to talk about our parts in daily conversations. "There's a part of me that wants to go out and meet my friends and a part of me that's happy to stay home." "There's a part of me that's worried about writing this book and a part of me that's excited to share my passion for Polyvagal Theory." When we are anchored in the regulating energy of our ventral vagal system, the following sentence can help us feel an internal sense of connection. Try filling in this sentence and see what inner connections you find: "There's a part of me that _____ and a part of me that _____."

Reflection practices strengthen our connection to self. The explorations in this book that take you inside to be with the many flavors of your autonomic experiences are a way of connecting. In addition to ongoing intentional practice, simply stopping during the day to take a moment just to be with yourself, to briefly turn inward and listen, builds those pathways of connection.

Connection with Others

Feel your social engagement system light up. If you want, you can place one hand on your heart and the other on the side of your face to find the pathways of this face-heart connection. Look out into the world and sense the ways you are connected with other people. Consider the ways you engage. You might connect remotely through text, email, phone, or video conference. You might have in-person connection through regularly scheduled activities or in-the-moment invitations. Take stock of the ways you connect at work, at play, at home, with family, and with friends.

As you consider the ways you come into connection, first think about what's working. Who are the people in your life with whom you feel a connection? What are the things you do together that foster that connection? Then explore what you might want to try. Who would you like to invite into connection? What would you do to explore making new connections?

Connection with the World

We connect with the world by the ways we inhabit our space and feel at home. We know we are home when we also know what it feels like to not be home. Through our nervous system, we have an embodied experience of home and not home. It's only when we experience both sides that we have a way to compare and contrast and recognize where we are.

When we listen to our nervous system, we can tune in to three stories. We can hear a story of being home in ventral safety and connection and two different stories of being away from home. One story of being away from home arises from the dorsal state of collapse and brings with it a sense of being homeless, forever lost in an unfamiliar land. The other story of being away from home comes out of intense sympathetic mobilization and activates a desperate search to find the way home. The story of being home is one of safety and connection that is guided by the flow of a regulated nervous system. This story is one of belonging. The poem "This Urge for Here" by my dear friend Gary Whited is to me a story of being home:

The sleeping dog by the stove,

the cardinal calling

in the maples out back,

that touch of wooden floor

on bare feet,

this taste of tea . . .

Oh urge grow deeper,

help me stay here.

Take some time to turn inward and listen to your three stories. How does your nervous system send you the message of feeling lost, unable to find the way home? What happens when you are frantically searching for the road home? And what is your embodied experience of coming home? Spend some time getting to know both sides of the experience—home and not home. Explore the feelings in your body, the words that accompany the feelings, and the actions you are drawn to from each experience.

No matter where we are in the world, we can take the feeling of being home with us. One of the ways I feel held in my story of home is a simple morning routine of drinking coffee and engaging in a morning conversation through text messages with a friend. It doesn't matter that we live in different parts of the country or that we travel to different time zones. I know she'll read my message with her morning coffee, just as I read hers with mine. Through this simple morning routine, I feel the predictability of co-regulation across time and space, and that brings me an embodied sense of home. What is a simple way that you experience home? As you look at your familiar routines is there one that carries the story of home?

In addition to our everyday story of home, I think we also have a more expansive experience of our soul feeling at home. When I've been away from the water for too long, there's an autonomic ache that's deep and persistent, and I know I have to find my way to the sea. Other people find their soul is at home in the forest, in the mountains, in the desert, or on the prairie. There are all sorts of environments that we call home. What is the environment that your soul needs to feel at home? How do you feel that experience of homecoming?

Connection with Spirit

While my connections to self, others, and the world are pretty stable, I find my connection to spirit continues to unfold. A number of years ago I was experiencing a moment of desperation. I was out of options and needed help, and in that moment, asked the Universe for guidance. I am not a religious person so what happened was surprising. Mother Mary showed up behind my right shoulder. I could see her and feel her presence and I was filled with a sense of awe. While the sense of her actual presence ebbs and flows, the energy stays with me and brings me the embodied knowing that I am not alone. What does a spiritual connection feel like to you? We connect in many ways including through spiritual beings, spirit animals, energetic beings, and ancestral connections. Invite a connection to spirit in whatever form it arrives for you in this moment.

Connection through each of the four pathways we've explored is one way to nourish the nervous system. We can think of this as filling our autonomic tanks. We need to know how full our tanks are, so to start, come up with an image for the gauge on your autonomic tank. Draw the gauge, mark the increments full, three quarters, half, a quarter, and empty, and then give each of the measures names that fit your experience. I use the image of the gas gauge in my car and label my increments full, filling, good enough, draining, and depleted.

Exploration:
Filling Your Autonomic Tank

Now that you have your image and words, use your gauge to explore how full your tank is. As you look at the four pathways of self, other, the world, and spirit where do you feel abundance and where do you feel longing? First consider the individual ways of connecting and identify where your gauge is for each. Which pathways are full or filling and which are heading toward empty? And now reflect on how your connection to self, others, the world, and spirit are working together to fill your autonomic tank. When you put the pathways together, where on your gauge are you? What are the combinations that are working and what are the connections your system is wanting in this moment? Take time to document what feels important for you to know and remember.

From Lonely to Connected

Pablo Neruda in "Ode and Burgeonings" wrote, "And one by one the nights between our separated cities are joined to the night that unites us." In today's world, we seem to be more focused on individuality and often assign more significance to our separateness than to our connections. We need to remember that our capacity to flourish on our own is built on a foundation of first being safely connected. And even as we move from co-regulation to self-regulation, we never lose the need to be safely connected with others. As long as we are alive, moments of both co-regulation and self-regulation are necessary for well-being.

> As long as we are alive, moments of both co-regulation and self-regulation are necessary for well-being.

We enter the world needing to co-regulate to survive and, with enough experiences of safety in co-regulation, we learn to self-regulate. Without the early experiences of safely co-regulating, self-regulating strategies are created as a survival response. While we might look like we are doing well, our internal experience is one of sympathetically driven fear. When we build a pattern of acting from a survival state, we suffer both physically and psychologically. We may be successful in the world, but we don't feel satisfied or find joy in our experiences.

Consider the ways you use self- and co-regulation. If you had people early in life who were predictably present and offered safe co-regulating experiences, it's more likely that your ability to self-regulate comes from a foundation of co-regulation. As you navigate your world you are reminded that you are safe and the world is a safe place to be, there are people you can count on, people you care about, and people to connect with. If you missed those safe, predictable, co-regulating experiences in your early life and haven't had enough experiences of that yet, it's more likely that you self-regulate from an autonomic state of survival. As you navigate your world from this place you think you are on your own, can't depend on others, and have to do it all by yourself.

Stephen Porges describes trauma as a chronic disruption of connectedness. The research tells us that experiences of connection and experiences of loneliness predict wellness, illness, and mortality. Studies show us that how connected or lonely we feel impacts the ways our body responds to viruses, the health of our hearts, our cognitive abilities, and even how long we live.[9] John Cacioppo, a pioneer in the research on loneliness, reminds us that humans are social beings and our nature is to recognize, interact, and form relationships with others.[10] Connection with others is about a sense of belonging and creating a shared sense of safety. Belonging is not just a psychological state, it's a biological need. Social connection is a necessary ingredient for a life of well-being.

One way to explore your experience of connection is with this short version of the UCLA loneliness scale.[11] On a scale of hardly ever, some of the time, and often, answer the following three questions:

1. How often do you feel that you lack companionship?

2. How often do you feel left out?

3. How often do you feel isolated from others?

Now score your answers: hardly ever = 1, some of the time = 2, often = 3. Total scores run along a continuum from 3 to 9, moving from least lonely to most lonely. While we don't need a scale to tell us what our nervous system knows, the numbers are an external validation and often an important acknowledgment of our experience.

Both social support and social connection are needed to help us meet the demands of our days. Social support comes from the people we count on to show up and help us in concrete ways and who make it possible for us to manage our daily living. These essential connections are formed around the exchange of services. When my husband had a stroke a number of years ago, he and I both appreciated the social support that brought some ease to our daily living. As you reflect on your daily living, who are your social supports?

Social connection, on the other hand, comes from the people in our life we know, and who know us, in deep ways. This is the person we call when we're feeling distressed and need someone to sit quietly with us without offering advice, the person who understands our need to rant sometimes and celebrates with us when life is good. Socially connected relationships are filled with reciprocity. With social connection we give and take, offer and receive. There is a rhythm to the relationship. As you reflect on your relationships, who is in the category of social connection for you? With whom do you feel that co-regulating, safe, predictable connection?

It is with enough experiences of social connection and ongoing, predictable opportunities for reciprocity and co-regulation that we create the foundation for self-regulation that sustains us when co-regulating experiences are not available.

Solitude

Unlike loneliness, solitude is a regulating and nourishing experience of choosing to be alone and feeling a sense of peace in that aloneness. In *The Way of Silence*, Brother David Steindl-Rast, Benedictine monk and beloved teacher on how to live in gratitude, reminds us that with strong roots in togetherness we can be solitary rather than lonely when we're alone:

Sometimes when we are alone, we find that—not so much in spite of but *because* of being so truly alone at that moment—we are united with everything and everybody. Whether we are alone [in our room or] with the trees, the rocks, the clouds, water, stars, wind, or whatever it is, we feel as if our heart is expanding, as if our being is expanding to embrace everything, as if the barriers were in some way broken down or dissolved, and we are one with all. When I am most truly alone, I am one with all.[12]

Without enough experiences of co-regulation, we can't find nourishment in solitude. Our unmet longing for connection either activates a desperate search for connection or prompts a collapse into despair and disconnection. Do you have enough experiences of co-regulation in your daily life so that you can also experience the sweetness of solitude?

Exploration: Solitude or Loneliness

It's important to know when we are savoring solitude and when we are moving into loneliness. What are the signs that you're shifting from feeling the peace of solitude and beginning to feel alone and lonely? I know I'm starting to move from solitude into loneliness when I begin to feel just a bit fuzzy, start to lose touch with my surroundings, and my thoughts turn from peace to worry.

Take a moment to explore what happens for you as you begin to leave the safety of solitude. Feel the ways your body sensations show you the beginning shift. Listen to your thoughts and identify the ones that point toward leaving ease and moving into loneliness. Turn toward your feelings and notice when they begin to shift from ones that live in your ventral state of safety and connection to those that emerge from sympathetic fear or dorsal despair.

Get to know your path between solitude and loneliness. Create the balance of experiences that meets your needs for being with others and supports your ability to savor moments of solitude.

From our first breath to our last, we are on a lifelong quest for connection. We are social beings with a biological need to connect and co-regulate with others. When this need is met, we can reach inward, connect to our own experience, and self-regulate. And from this platform of safety in self- and co-regulation, we are able to connect with the world around us and with spirit to guide us.

5

Neuroception: Your Nervous System's Intuition

We have all a better guide in ourselves, if we would
attend to it, than any other person can be.

JANE AUSTEN,
MANSFIELD PARK

We first touched on neuroception in chapter 1 as one of the organizing principles of Polyvagal Theory. Building on that brief introduction, let's now explore in more detail what neuroception is and how it works.

Intuition is our ability to know something without thinking about it or using facts to understand it. We can think of neuroception as our autonomic intuition. Because the autonomic nervous system is a system that works mostly outside of our awareness and operates below the level of our thinking brain, neuroception is a way of knowing that is very different from our cognitive understanding. Through the process of neuroception, the nervous system listens to what's happening in our embodied, environmental, and relational experiences, looks for cues of safety and danger, and responds by shutting down, mobilizing for action, or anchoring in regulation. While we like to think we are using our wise and wonderful brains to make decisions, in fact, long before information reaches the brain, the autonomic nervous system takes action.

Without awareness, neuroception works in the background serving our survival and shaping our days. It is when we bring perception to neuroception that we have access to perspective. By adding perception to the autonomic process of neuroception, we are no longer simply in the state; we are now able to be with it and observe and reflect on the experience. Eighty percent of the information coming from our vagal pathways flows from the body to the brain in what we call afferent pathways, while 20 percent returns from the brain to the body in what we call efferent pathways. (An easy way to remember the two terms is afferent arrives and efferent exits.) The brain takes the information that it receives from the body and turns it into a story to make sense of what's happening in the body. When we bring perception to neuroception and bring awareness to the three streams of autonomic information (embodied, environmental, and relational), we invite the body and the brain to work together. Then we become more than simple story listeners. We become story editors and story writers.

Through neuroception, the nervous system listens as we move through our days, continuously assessing risk and responding in service of survival. We are aware of our responses first on a physical level, then through connection with the story that emerges. Sometimes the impact is hidden, experienced on the inside and known only to us. We feel shifts in our breathing and heartbeat, changes in our digestion, and different sensations in our throat. Our thoughts begin to form a story. This internal experience is often accompanied by an impulse to take action. At other times our responses are visible to the world. Our facial expressions, tone of voice, gestures, and posture show others what we are feeling. We say what we are thinking and the impulse to take action that was hidden on the inside comes alive and is now seen in our behaviors.

Our autonomic nervous system often moves in a way that helps us successfully manage an experience. For example, I'm anchored in regulation as I enjoy a walk in the woods and mobilize when I see a snake on the path. Neuroception is a match for what is happening in the moment, accurately answering the question, "Am I safe?" We can also feel alarmed and hyper-vigilant when there is no actual risk. I might feel highly anxious whenever I answer my phone or be acutely aware of every sound and need to know exactly where it's coming from. Or we can experience the world in a dulled and unaware state. I don't pay attention to where I'm walking and always bump into things, or I don't recognize when someone reaches out in friendship. When these kinds of alarmed or unaware experiences happen, we could say our nervous system isn't accurately attending to the question of safety and moves in a way that is a mismatch.

Sometimes we ignore or override our neuroception. See if you can remember a time when your neuroception sent you a message and you didn't listen—maybe you felt reluctant to accept an invitation and did it anyway—or a time when you listened but didn't follow that guidance. Perhaps you felt in your heart you shouldn't agree to work on a project and dismissed it as a foolish feeling and said yes. When we don't listen, or when we listen and discount the information, we often regret it later. We look back and realize that our autonomic nervous system was sending an important message, and in that moment we weren't able, or ready, to take in the information and use it for our well-being.

Childhood is when we begin to learn to tune in or tune out. We are taught to listen and be guided by what we hear or to ignore and override the messages neuroception is sending. We may have grown up in homes where we were told that what we felt wasn't okay, wasn't right, and to ignore what our neuroception was telling us. In this environment we were trained to not listen and to not pay attention. Or we may have been helped early in life to tune in to our feelings and take them into account when making decisions. The people around us taught us it was safe to look at the world and talk about what we saw. In this environment we learned that our internal experience has important information.

Exploration:
Shaping Neuroception

Take a moment to reflect on your experience. Were you taught to honor or ignore your neuroception? Begin your sentence with "In my family . . . ." Think about what you learned growing up in your family and fill in the rest of the sentence. If you were taught to tune in to your neurocep-tion, you might say, "In my family it was safe to say what I was feeling." If you were taught to ignore your neuroception your sentence might be, "In my family people pretended nothing was hap-pening, and it was safer not to have a feeling." Write several sentences to get to know the ways your family shaped your ability to use information from neuroception to guide your daily living.

> Reclaiming the power to listen and learning to tune in to the wisdom of the nervous system is part of living a life of well-being.

Reclaiming the power to listen and learning to tune in to the wisdom of the nervous system is part of living a life of well-being. For this we move from the past to the present. Using the same sentences, change *my*, which represents what we learned growing up, to *this*, which represents the way we are living now. These new sentences give us the opportunity to look at the ways connecting to our inner wisdom is supported or not supported by the people who are present in our lives now.

If the people you consider family value connecting to neu-roception and the embodied, environmental, and relational information it sends, write "In this family . . ." sentences to clearly describe the ways that it is practiced. Your sen-tences will bring awareness to the ways you are supported in tuning in and remind you to keep listening. If listening to neuroception is not something that is encouraged by the people around you, write sentences that describe the values you intend to create. These sentences will help serve as a reminder of the conditions you are committing to creating in your life that make it possible to follow the wisdom of your nervous system.

There's a difference between being unaware of the ways we are guided by the nervous system and the decision to override the direction our nervous system is pointing us toward. Sometimes we have to approach an experience even when our neuroception is sending cues of danger. We have a medical concern to follow up on, need to confront a colleague with a work issue, or need to set limits in a friendship. When we stay tuned in instead of turning away, we can acknowledge the cues of danger, look for ways to reduce them, and make an intentional choice to move forward in the direction that may still be scary but is necessary.

Recently one of my reliable ventral anchoring practices has been impacted by a change in neuroception. I have a medical issue involving my heart that is being monitored, and like most people, when confronted with a health challenge my neuroception is not one of safety. Since many of the practices that help me anchor in regulation include placing a hand on my heart, I often bump into awareness of my medical condition. Now, rather than a reassuring cue of safety, my neuroception activates a cue of danger, and I get pulled into anxiety. What used to be a soothing practice has become a more complicated experience. When I touch my heart area, I begin to worry about my heart rhythms. What I've found is that I can reduce the neuroception of danger by feeling my heartbeat and imagining my valves working, and then my familiar hand-on-heart practice once again helps me anchor in ventral safety.

The neuroception of danger around my health also challenges my ability to move forward with tests and treatment. Thinking about scheduling an appointment brings a cue of danger. I'm quickly pulled into sympathetic flight, and the intensity of my survival response makes it difficult for me to take action. Acknowledging that the medical challenge is real and treatment does include risk allows me to tune in and get clear about the cues of danger. Making a list of steps to follow and giving myself permission to move one step at a time helps. Talking with people who have already had these tests and treatment brings me a sense of not being alone in a scary process. While I can't fully resolve the neuroception of danger, I am finding a way to work with my nervous system.

Exploration: Safe Enough

It is natural to have things in our lives that feel a bit scary and that we still want, or need, to engage with. This might be a resource you've been using that has now become complicated or a difficult situation you need to address. Start by identifying an experience you want to explore. Now gather the information you need to move forward. Turn toward the experience and listen to the cues of danger. Take time to really hear what your nervous system wants you to know. Having listened, how do you connect what you learned with what you need to do in a way that brings safety? If you're working with a resource, experiment with steps you can take to reduce the cues of danger and reconnect with the regulating influence of the practice. If you're exploring a difficult situation, noticing and naming cues of danger begins to soften them a bit, making it possible to make a plan to work with them. Look for cues of safety that might already be present or cues that you could bring in. Discover what needs to happen so you can honor your survival response and work with your nervous system to take the next steps.

Tuning In

We can think of neuroception as an embodied surveillance system broadcasting important information from its place below the surface of awareness. When we connect to this information system, we can use the messages to inform our decisions. When you tune in, where in your body do you find your surveillance system? We often think of a gut instinct and many people do feel that instinct, or what I like to think of as our autonomic intuition, in their gut, but you might locate yours in another place. Touch that place with a hand or direct your attention there. Notice what changes as you bring awareness to what is normally an unconscious experience.

Now that you have this connection to your embodied surveillance system, see if there is an image to represent it. Some of the images people use include a lighthouse with a beacon that revolves, a guard standing in a watchtower, a gentle watchdog who's always ready to respond, and a ball of light that changes color. To see what your inner surveillance system looks like, focus on the place in your body where you located it, invite an image, and wait to see what emerges. Stay open to what comes. We can be surprised by the creativity of our internal world to bring our autonomic experiences to life. When you have the image, spend some time getting to know how it works. How does it track moment to moment cues of safety and danger?

In the beginning, as you get to know the ways your neuroception works, it can be interesting or even a bit alarming to tune in to the stream of information that's always flowing beneath our conscious awareness. We're used to paying attention to our thoughts, feelings, and behaviors, but we're not used to being curious about what's underneath and discovering what our autonomic nervous system is hearing. To support this new way of listening, we first need to create a pathway that's easy to travel and lets us connect with the original cue that sparked an experience.

Exploration: Building an Information Pathway

Neuroception begins the creation of our behaviors, our feelings, and our stories. When we intentionally find our way to that starting point, we can bring what otherwise remains hidden into awareness. To create a pathway to bring together neuroception and perception, the first move is from outer awareness to inner connection. Turn toward your inner world and find the place you identified earlier where neuroception reaches out for your attention. Now move to finding the place where you feel your perception. Because this involves the cortex and the thinking parts of our brains, many people locate their place of perception somewhere inside the head. Again take time to find your personal place of perception.

With the two individual locations of neuroception and perception identified, the next step is to connect them. With a pathway between neuroception and perception, the cues of safety and danger that emerge can travel easily into your awareness, and you can also follow your actions, feelings, and stories back to their autonomic origins. It may be helpful to put your hands on the two locations as you begin to imagine the route from neuroception to awareness. The pathway you imagine might be a straight line between the two points or a more circuitous route. Whatever shape the connection takes, the essential quality is to support the easy, reliable transmission of information. My neuroception-to-perception pathway is marked by curves and loops in its route from the center of my chest to my forehead. Take time to let the shape of your route become clear.

To practice, first think of a behavior you're curious about and imagine enacting it. Move from perception to the neuroception that is underneath the behavior. Follow the pathway you identified that connects your two embodied points. As I travel my circuitous route from my forehead to my chest, I feel the twists and turns. When you arrive at the place of neuroception, take a moment to sense the cue of safety or danger. Do the same for a feeling you're interested in. And finally, bring to mind a story about yourself or the world that you'd like to learn more about and activate your perception connection. What's underneath this story? And now travel the pathway in the opposite direction. Come into connection with the first stirrings of a sense of safety or danger and see where that takes you. Follow the beginning of an embodied cue into a feeling, a thought, an action, and then a story.

As you use this new way of moving between information systems, the pathway becomes stronger. To strengthen the connection, create a way to tune in and intentionally engage. Experiment with a variety of ways to see what works for you. Draw the pathway and trace it with your finger as you move between these two ways of knowing. Place a hand on your body as a physical reminder of this internal pathway. Create an intention to activate the pathway in both directions during the flow of your day. Make a plan to reflect at the end of the day and see how neuroception took you to a particular behavior, feeling, or story. Stop when you notice the emergence of a behavior, feeling, or story and follow the path from perception to neuroception. What are the ways you want to attend to this new pathway?

Some responses are what I call factory-installed settings. We generally respond in similar ways to certain sounds. With high frequencies, we look toward the sound, sensing it as a distress call. Low frequencies remind us of predators and prompt an urge to get away. And sounds in the range of a human voice invite us into safety and connection. Other cues are shaped by our personal histories and may be similar or very different from the people around us. I grew up with a father who loved loud classical music and, for me, the feeling of being surrounded by loud music feels regulating and connecting. For other people, loud music activates a neuroception of danger. You can probably recognize a cue that elicits a very different response for you than for your friends. Take a moment and identify a cue that brings a neuroception of safety to you but not the people around you. And now the opposite, something that activates a neuroception of danger for you while people around you find the same experience creates a neuroception of safety. Although we all share common autonomic pathways between safety and danger, we each have our own response patterns.

Exploration:
Awareness of Neuroception

The Moment of Change

Sometimes neuroception brings a dramatic change to our state, and we feel the intensity both in our bodies and our stories. You can explore this by thinking of a time when you felt a large state shift that moved you out of safety into danger. Maybe you were startled by a sound and felt your body respond in fear, or someone walked away from you and you felt yourself shutting down. As you reflect on the shift from safety to danger, see if you can identify the moment when you felt the change in your body and then how your story changed. Then find a time when your state changed in the other direction, from danger back to safety. Perhaps you saw a friendly face or heard a familiar sound and felt a return of ease. Again look for the moment when you felt that happen and see how the story that accompanied it began to change.

At other times, we have a more nuanced experience of change. We feel a subtle shift in the intensity of a state. You might feel worry moving into anxiety, frustration becoming anger, or lack of focus leading to checking out. When we attend to these micro-shifts, we can fine-tune our ability to track the subtle shifts that happen within states. Tuning in to this can help us understand how small shifts within a state can eventually lead to a movement between states.

Noticing Cues

With this beginning awareness, let's move deeper into bringing perception to neuroception. Stop for a moment and bring your attention to the three streams of neuroception—embodied, environmental, and relational—that are at work in this present moment. Use the following questions to consider the information your neuroception is taking in:

What are the cues of danger in this moment in your body? Start with a simple body scan. Is there an ache, tension, soreness, or numbness? Listen to your digestion, heart rate, and breath. Let your body show you cues of danger.

What are the cues of safety in this moment in your body? Listen to your body. Find the places of ease, warmth, and flexibility. Feel your heart and breath rhythms. Let your body show you cues of safety.

What are the cues of danger in this moment in the immediate environment around you? Bring your awareness to the space you are inhabiting. Look around and see what is distressing.

Move your awareness out into the larger environment. As you look outside your space to the world around you, what do you find that feels distressing?

What are the cues of safety in this moment in the immediate environment around you? Bring your awareness back to the space you are in. Look around and see what brings you some joy. Find what helps you anchor in regulation.

And now move your awareness out into the larger environment. As you look outside your space to the world around you, what do you find that feels nourishing?

What are the cues of danger in this moment in your connection with others? Look for signs of warning your social engagement system is sending or receiving from someone's eyes, facial expression, tone of voice, posture, and movements.

What are the cues of safety in this moment in your connection with others? Look for the signs of welcome your social engagement system is sending or receiving from someone's eyes, facial expression, tone of voice, posture, and movements.

When we explore our experiences of neuroception, we want to stay curious about what we find. A response that feels out of proportion to the present-moment situation, a reaction that is too big or too constrained, often points to a familiar cue from the past that's being touched in the present. Feeling overwhelming anger at a small interruption while you're working or feeling numb when someone tells you they appreciate something you've done might point to an experience from the past coming alive in the present. Other responses feel like they're grounded in the present and move us toward or away from people, places, or things not because of a past experience but in response to our neuroception in the moment. For example, you get an email from a friend and feel the invitation to connect, or you think about a big work project and feel a bit anxious.

It's important to know whether our responses are coming from the past or are grounded in the present. To do this, we can use a clarifying question. First, bring perception to the present moment. What cues are you getting right now? Is your neuroception one of safety or danger? And now ask the question, "In this moment, in this place, with this person or these people, is this response (or this intensity of response) needed?" Notice we ask if the response is needed, not if it is appropriate. Categories of appropriate or not appropriate, good and bad, don't apply. The autonomic nervous system doesn't make meaning or assign motivation. It simply takes in cues and enacts the response it deems necessary to ensure survival. If the answer to the clarifying question is yes, you're likely anchored in the present moment and your response can be a useful guide in making decisions. If the answer is no, look for a familiar cue that has reached out from your past and taken hold in the present. Think about other times in your life when you have felt this way. Look for the cues of danger that are similar between the past and now. When we find the thread that connects experiences, we have new information to help us understand our patterns.

Safety is essential for survival, but to our nervous system, not being in danger is not the same as being safe. Being out of danger doesn't guarantee we experience a neuroception of safety. The systems that have been put in place to create safety impact how we communicate and shape the ways we create connection. Security procedures in schools and screenings at airports and train stations may concretely add layers of safety but be experienced through our neuroception as cues of danger. In the time of a global pandemic, disconnection through plexiglass partitions separating people, rules around social distancing, and required wearing of face masks may be necessary to help us stay safe but do not necessarily engender a neuroception of safety.

Think about the systems you regularly interact with. What are the cues of safety and danger that you feel as you navigate through these systems? You'll recognize cues of safety in the ways you feel alive and anchored in regulation and cues of danger in the ways your sympathetic and dorsal survival states activate. Bring perception to these experiences and see where your neuroception takes you.

In order to find well-being we need to attend to cues of both danger and safety. We need to reduce or resolve cues of danger and actively experience cues of safety. One without the other doesn't bring us to well-being. To explore this, think of a particular experience that feels just a little unsafe or holds just a hint of distress. Start by bringing perception to neuroception and identify the specific cues of danger that you feel. Use the three streams of neuroception to look for cues inside your body, outside in the environment, and between you and others. When you identify a cue of danger, consider how you might reduce it or if there is a way to resolve it. What is possible? Experiences often include more than one cue of danger. Stop and explore each one you find.

And now move your attention to cues of safety. Take time to see what embodied, environmental, and relational cues of safety are present in the experience. We humans are built with a negativity bias to help ensure our survival. Because of this, we are on the lookout for cues of danger and often miss the cues of safety. Look back on the experience and see if there are any cues of safety you might have missed. Next bring some curiosity to exploring what cues of safety it might be possible to bring in.

Awareness is the active ingredient needed to work with neuroception. To engage with your inner surveillance system and learn to use it wisely, bring awareness to the cues of danger and make an intention to connect with cues of safety. With awareness we can explore with curiosity and create the conditions necessary to create an embodied sense of safety in our daily living experiences.

6

Patterns of Connection
and Protection

Life is a pattern of energies.

BAKER BROWNELL,
THE NEW UNIVERSE

O ur autonomic patterns are shaped by the environments we
inhabit and the people we're in relationship with. Cues of safety
deepen our feeling of connection while cues of danger pull us out of
feeling anchored in our lives. The nervous system takes these cues and
builds the pathways of connection and protection that we travel as we
make our way through the day. Although the nervous system is shaped
by our past experiences, it never stops taking in cues and updating
the pathways. As we learn to attend to the world and our habitual
responses, we begin to get to know the ways our patterns of connection and protection stay quiet or come alive.

The nervous system uses pathways of connection and protection
to help us survive traumatic moments and to navigate the ordinary
challenges of daily life. The myriad moments we have experienced,
from loving and joy filled to scary and hurtful, are woven together
and create a particular design. Depending on our personal histories,
we build stronger patterns of connection or stronger patterns of protection. The good news is that no matter how the nervous system has
been shaped, the capacity for moving out of protection and returning
to connection is built into our biology.

At the top of the hierarchy, anchored in safety and regulation, is the place where we find physical and psychological well-being and experience health, growth, and restoration. I call this our autonomic home. Look back to your exploration in chapter 2 and review what your landscape looked like from your home in ventral. Connection brings us home, and protection takes us to our home away from home in sympathetic mobilization or dorsal shutdown. While we move in and out of both survival states, with repeated activation we create our own protection profile. Over time, our habitual survival response leans more toward mobilization and fight and flight or disconnection and shutdown. Then when a pattern of protection is needed, we are easily transported to this home away from home.

Exploration: Finding Your Home Away from Home

My home away from home is rooted in dorsal disconnection. When I feel too many cues of danger, I take an internal step back. It's not as intense a response as it used to be and often goes unnoticed by the people around me, but in that moment I'm no longer able to fully connect and I feel that loss. Take a moment and consider how you make your way through the world. Where is your home away from home? When you leave connection and get pulled into a pattern of protection, where do you usually end up? Do you ride out the cues of danger in the intense charge of your sympathetic action-taking system, or are you rescued by disappearing into dorsal shutdown? As you find your home away from home, bring curiosity to looking at the ways your survival response is working to protect you. Ask yourself, if you weren't under the protection of your home away from home, what might be happening? You can explore your stories with if-then statements. For example, "If I didn't feel so anxious or angry right now, then I would _____" or "If I begin to be seen and connect with the world, then _____." Write your own if-then statements and get to know how your nervous system is working to protect you.

Understanding the biology of connection and protection offers us hope. Our early experiences shaped our systems, and our ongoing experiences continue to shape them. When we identify what moves us into protection, we can explore how to reduce those experiences and create more moments of connection. And when we discover the present-day experiences that shape our system toward connection, we can engage with them more often and deepen the pattern.

Whenever we think about patterns of protection and talk about survival responses, we want to add the word *adaptive*. As crazy, incongruous, or inexplicable as our thoughts, feelings, or actions may seem, we need to remember the autonomic nervous system is always working to ensure our survival. While it often doesn't make cognitive sense, the nervous system feels a need and takes action. It's by looking through that lens at our own responses and at the responses of the people around us that we are able to avoid becoming critical and remain curious. And then curiosity opens the door to compassion and self-compassion.

Think of a time when you moved into an adaptive survival response, a moment of protection that brought you into mobilization or shutdown. From a place of curiosity, spend a moment and explore the adaptive survival response. What did your nervous system sense? How did the survival response protect you? Now remember a time when someone around you moved into their own adaptive survival response. Bring some curiosity to what was going on for them.

Looking at adaptive survival responses, whether our own or someone else's, with curiosity can be challenging. When we are learning to look through the lens of the nervous system, it is easy to move out of curiosity into self-judgment and self-criticism. I've found that an easy way to bring some self-compassion is by adding one of my favorite words: *yet*. *Yet* holds a feeling of change and a sense of possibility. "I can't be curious about the story I'm telling myself yet." "I'm not able to look at other people without judging their behaviors yet." Make a statement, add *yet* to the end of the sentence, and see what happens.

When we see that stories and actions are based in biology, we remember that what we label as motivation is simply an autonomic intention for survival. We humans make moral meaning and assign intent, but the autonomic nervous system doesn't think in terms of good or bad, it simply acts in service of survival. It's a different experience once you recognize that the friend who has just stopped listening to you still wants to be in connection, but their biology is making it impossible for them to stay present and listen. Or when your child isn't listening, it's not because he is defiant but because he is unable to regulate. When we remember to look beyond behaviors to see the state, it's easier to stay anchored in regulation, not respond from our own pattern of protection, and reach out to offer connection.

Bring to mind a person you care about and who is having a difficult time. Look at them through the lens of their nervous system. What do you see? Where has their nervous system taken them? How does this influence what you want to do? And now bring to mind a person who you struggle to be in connection with. Put aside the story you've created and look through the lens of the nervous system. What state do you imagine they are being held in? Does this help you find some curiosity or compassion?

We label people in lots of ways. We say they don't care, they're not trying, they don't want to change, or they're lazy, irresponsible, always angry, or unreliable. What if instead of using these labels we thought about people as being dysregulated? Behavior makes sense when we look at it through the autonomic state. When someone is pulled into the mobilizing energy of sympathetic fight and flight or trapped in dorsal shutdown, their biology doesn't support them coming into connection and co-regulating or using healthy strategies of self-regulation. When we recognize an adaptive survival response, our own or someone else's, instead of a story about motive and meaning, we can listen to the story of a neuroception of danger and an autonomic nervous system that is reacting to a need for protection.

A Connection/Protection Equation

I use a simple equation to think about moving between connection and protection. When the cues of safety outweigh the cues of danger, we move to connect, and when the cues of danger outweigh the cues of safety, we take actions to protect. Sometimes this is felt in the number of cues. There are simply more cues of safety or danger. Other times the intensity of one particular cue can counteract several others. The cue of safety from someone sending a smile might outweigh being in an environment with several cues of danger. Because the nervous system is continuously taking in cues, the safety/danger equation is always changing. As the number of cues or strength of cues changes, the equation shifts, affecting our bodies, behaviors, and stories. When the connection side is greater than the protection side, we are anchored in safety and regulation, ready to reach out and explore. Our stories are ones of hope and possibility. When the protection side is greater than the connection side, we are either highly mobilized or pulled into collapse. We lose our curiosity and instead see the world as unsafe. Our stories reflect the danger or disinterest we feel.

Take a moment to experiment with your personal connection/protection equation. Feel what it's like for you when the cues of safety outweigh the cues of danger. Start by noticing what happens in your body. Then look at some of your feelings. And finally, bring awareness to the story that emerges.

Now, feel what happens as the balance starts to tip and the cues of danger add up and begin to prevail over the cues of safety. Feel what happens as you begin to move into mobilization or get pulled into shutdown. Start with your body and notice the response, then see what feelings you find, and finally listen to the stories that emerge.

Exploration:
Connecting with Cues

As we begin to understand these basic ingredients, we can move to the next step and identify the cues of safety and danger that change the equation. The goal is to clearly identify the cues that pull us toward something, someone, or some place, inviting connection, and the cues that propel us away, activating protection. We need to bring attention to the cues that are in the background, tucked away out of awareness where they powerfully impact our capacity for connection.

Staying in curiosity and out of self-criticism is the key to this exploration. We need an anchor in regulation to be curious and not judgmental. You might connect by putting your hand on the place in your body where you discovered your ventral vagal system comes alive, returning to your ventral landscape, or moving to an actual place in your environment that helps you come into a ventral state.

Feeling Cues

Start by exploring how you feel the cues. How do you know when your neuroception is one of safety? Think of an experience that brings you a wish to move closer, to engage and connect. What happens in your body? What are your feelings? What do you want to do here? And what is the story that you hear? When my neuroception is one of safety, my body takes on a sense of being open. The world interests me, and I'm ready to engage and explore. My stories are filled with possibilities and options.

Next explore an experience that fills you with anger or anxiety and makes you want to argue or run away. Get to know these cues of danger. What happens in your body? What are your feelings? What do you want to do here? And what is the story that you hear? From this flavor of danger my body feels tense, I'm filled with worry, and I have an unrelenting need to manage the people and things in my world. My stories are now ones of being trapped in a chaotic world.

And finally explore an experience that overwhelms you and brings the need to shut down and disconnect. What happens in your body now? What are you feeling? What do you want to do? And what's the story you hear? When I feel the pull toward shutdown, the energy drains from my body and I begin to lose hope. My story is one of giving up and believing it's not worth trying and nothing is ever going to change.

Receiving Cues

Now that we know more about how we feel cues, the next step is to identify when we feel them. Can you notice the moment when you feel a cue of safety or danger? What sign does your nervous system send you that a cue has arrived? Let's start at the bottom of the hierarchy. Think of a recent interaction, and look for the moment when a cue of danger appeared and you were pulled into shutdown. Get to know the ways your nervous system sends you that information. Perhaps you feel something happening in your body. Maybe a movement emerges, you hear words, or an image appears. Move up one step on the hierarchy and do the same for a recent interaction that took you into fight and flight. Get to know the ways your nervous system sends you this information. And finally, end at the top of the hierarchy and reflect on a recent interaction with a cue of safety and the messages your nervous system sends. Use your journal to document what you discovered about the ways you feel cues of safety and danger arriving in your system.

Understanding Cues

With the ability to tune in to the experiences that flow from neuroception and identify how and when we receive cues, we can now turn to considering what those cues are. Return to the interactions you just used to identify cues of danger and safety and begin to look at the specific cues you came into connection with. Start with the cues of danger that took you into shutdown. What is it in the experience that brings this move into protection? Is there a sound? Is there something in particular you see, a tone of voice, or a look on someone's face?

As you move into protection, what are the words you hear? Is there a belief that arises? Stop here and take time to document what you've discovered.

Next return to the other experience of danger and explore the cues that bring the move into mobilization and the energy of fight and flight. Again look for a sound, something in particular you see, a tone of voice, a look on someone's face, words you hear, or a belief that appears. Document the specific cues that move you into this state of protection.

Now turn to the experience that was filled with cues of safety. What is it in the experience that brings a move into connection? Is there something in the environment? With another person? As you move into connection, what words do you hear? Is there a belief that emerges here? Again, stop and document what you've discovered.

Finding Patterns

As we explore what moves us into protection or connection, we begin to look for patterns. Are there certain tones of voice or facial expressions or words that invite connection or activate protection? For most people a face with a smile brings a pattern of connection, and a face without expression activates a pattern of protection. Are there certain sounds? The sound of the sea automatically brings me into connection while the sound of lots of people talking activates a move into protection. How about the environment? For me, a seascape invites me into connection while a cityscape takes me to protection.

Bring your attention to people and pets. There are certain people in our lives who bring cues of safety while other people activate cues of danger. Combinations of people often do the same. Large groups of people tend to activate my pattern of protection, while groups of three or four offer a safe invitation for connection. Pets have been shown to predictably bring alive patterns of connection, so if people are cues of danger for you, a pet can bring a safe sense of mammal-to-mammal connection. Take time to explore your responses. As we get to know our particular patterns, to know the elements that move us toward and away, we can use this information to create an equation where the cues of safety outweigh the cues of danger.

Building a Flexible System

We know that well-being is an outcome of a flexible autonomic nervous system. We will all at times be pulled into patterns of protection and struggle to find our way back to connection. But as we increase our ability to move between patterns of protection and patterns of connection and not get stuck in protection, we build flexibility. Flexibility is tied to resilience. Resilience is an outcome of a nervous system that moves from patterns of connection to protection and back to connection with some ease. A way to measure our level of resilience is by tracking how often we get pulled into protection, how long we stay there, and how easily we can find our way back into connection.

> Resilience is an outcome of a nervous system that moves from patterns of connection to protection and back to connection with some ease.

Exploration:
Getting Unstuck

Listen

First, find your anchor in safety and then set the intention to explore an experience of being stuck in a survival state. Think of a situation that's activated one of your survival responses. See where you are stuck, unable to move out of a place of mobilization or shutdown even though you really want to. Listen to the story you're telling yourself. Remember information is traveling the body-to-brain pathways. It's your brain's job to make sense of what's happening in your body, so the brain creates a story filled with motive and meaning. The story is often one of blame, criticism, and judgment of ourselves or others. As you explore, remind yourself to just listen. This is an information-gathering step, not a time to make changes.

Be Curious

Now that you've heard the brain's story, turn toward your autonomic story. To do this, first notice the survival state and then name it. When you look through the lens of your nervous system, where are you? Mobilized or shut down? Remind yourself that this response is activated because the connection/protection equation is out of balance. Your biology has reacted to a neuroception of danger. Remembering that and naming your experience in this way begins the process of letting go of judgment and self-blame and making room for curiosity. As you turn toward your state, listen to the story your nervous system tells. Look for the ways this story is similar to or different from the one your brain creates.

Change the Equation

We know we're taken out of connection into protection when the cues of danger outweigh the cues of safety. Bring your attention to identifying the cues of danger. Can you reduce or resolve any of them? Then explore adding cues of safety. What might be possible to bring into the experience? Play with this until you find the combination of cues that begins to move your system out of the pattern of protection and back into a state of connection, back into enough safety to get unstuck.

See What Emerges

An emergent property of being anchored in safety and regulation is the ability to move ahead, find options, and creatively solve problems. What happens as you shift the balance in your equation? What changes when the cues of safety begin to outweigh the cues of danger? Bring curiosity to the change in your state and the autonomic and cognitive stories that accompany that change.

Moving Between

Sometimes our states work in harmony. When our ventral state holds the space for our sympathetic and dorsal states to play their important roles, the path between the states is easy to travel, and the experience is one of well-being. At other times our sympathetic or dorsal states take over, and the path becomes more challenging. The following meditation, which I first introduced in my book *The Polyvagal Theory in Therapy*, is a way to begin to get to know your pathways of connection and protection.

Just as an anchor holds a ship safely, you can anchor in your ventral vagal state. Feel yourself rooted in the energy of safety this system offers. Your breath is full, and each exhalation moves you along the pathway that supports safety and connection. There's a rhythm to your heart rate and this beat brings well-being. You're held in the autonomic safety circuit—your body-to-brain pathway sends messages of stability, and the returning brain-to-body pathway creates a story of safety. From this foundation of safety, with the sense of your anchor being firmly planted in your ventral vagal system, you can begin the journey to explore your sympathetic and dorsal vagal responses.

First reach into the mobilized energy of the sympathetic nervous system. Feel your breath change and your heart rate speed up. You might want to move, and your thoughts may begin to swirl. Imagine the sympathetic sea and the energy that moves here, mobilizing your system toward action. Perhaps you can feel the wind blowing, disturbing the sea, and sense the waves, rolling breakers, and crashing surf. Notice that you can safely navigate this sympathetic storm; you're tethered to your safety circuit. Remember that your anchor is deeply dug into the firm ground of ventral vagal regulation.

Return to the place where you first set your anchor. Feel into the regulating energies of breath and heart rate, feel the flow of warmth in your chest, and sense the solid ground beneath you. Your ventral vagal system is sending you signals of safety.

And now gently begin the descent into the dorsal vagal state. This is not the dorsal dive that can take you out of present time awareness into numbness. This is just an experimental dipping of your toe into the feeling of disconnection. Energy might begin to drain from your body, and everything might start to slow down. You might feel a restriction of movement. Manage this experience by bringing active remembrance of your connection to your ventral vagal state, the place you first set your anchor. Feel those regulating energies controlling the depth and the speed of your dorsal vagal descent. You're moving along a slope, not plummeting into space. Your anchor is secure, holding your place in ventral vagal regulation, allowing you to safely explore the dorsal vagal experience.

And now come back once more to where you started in ventral vagal regulation; return to where you set your anchor. Savor the ways you can befriend your sympathetic nervous system and dorsal vagal responses when you're guided by your autonomic safety circuit.

Exploration: Traveling Regulated Pathways

Having used the meditation above as a beginning guide for moving between states, we can now explore the pathways that help us move between states with safety and ease. Start by imagining the route you follow when your three states are connected and working together. The ventral state is regulating your system while the sympathetic and dorsal states work in the background. The sympathetic system brings you the energy needed to move through the day, and the dorsal system regulates your digestion, bringing you nutrients to nourish you. This is the state of healthy homeostasis, the place of well-being. You're anchored in regulation and traveling with a sense of safety. You might see an actual path to walk, a rope to hold on to, or a ladder to climb. Maybe you take an elevator or ride a stream of light. Take time to find your own unique route between states.

Now experiment with traveling your personal pathway. Imagine moving through the states from ventral to sympathetic to dorsal and back through sympathetic to ventral again. Notice how your pathway supports you in moving between states with flexibility and ease. Change your image in any way that you need to feel fully safe and supported. Take some time to document the regulated pathway that leads you safely between slow, dorsal nourishment, sympathetic excitement, and the flow of ventral connection. Many people find some form of illustration or a combination of art and words is helpful when documenting these pathways.

Exploration:
Navigating Pathways of Protection

With the experience of moving through a regulated system using your pathway image, we can begin to explore how to safely travel between states when we're challenged by sympathetic energy and dorsal protection. First let's explore the pathway downward out of connection and find what keeps you from free-falling into a sympathetic state and then plummeting to dorsal. How do you slow the descent? You can use your regulated pathway and add details to safeguard your journey. You might want resting places along the path, a railing or handholds, more stopping points in an elevator, or more shades of color in a light stream. Sometimes the path through protection is totally different from the path through regulation. Your gentle trail to walk could turn into a cliff to scale. Turn inward, take time to listen, and let your nervous system show you the pathway that leads downward out of connection and the elements that help you safely make that journey.

Having explored how to regulate the move out of connection down through the two states of protection, let's now look at the mechanics of traveling the pathway in reverse. Coming out of dorsal immobilization to connect with some sympathetic mobilizing energy is challenging to do on our own. We often need help with that beginning movement upward. Maybe there's a button you push to begin the ascent, a stream of light that helps you begin to beam up, or a hand that reaches out to you. Take the time you need to let your nervous system send you the image.

To continue the journey upward to ventral connection, we need to connect with the mobilizing energy in an organized way. Without a way to safely connect with the energy, we will either stay stuck here or take the path back to dorsal. What is needed here to support you in using this energy as a resource to keep you heading up into ventral regulation? This might be a continuation of the element that began the ascent from dorsal or it might be something new. Find the element that keeps you moving and helps you stay on track.

Now that you've discovered the essential elements of your pathways out of safety into survival and back to safety, go ahead and make the trek down and back. Use these pathways and become comfortable with how they work and confident in your ability to travel them. Each time you do this, you strengthen your ability to move from connection to protection and back again. These are the pathways that help you manage your move out of connection into protection and guide you home to safety and regulation and the possibilities that come from being anchored in ventral state. Take time to document what you discovered.

Exploration:
Appreciating Our Home
Away from Home

When we work with our patterns of protection from an anchor in regulation, we can understand and appreciate the ways our autonomic nervous system acts in service of our survival. To safely explore your home away from home, the place your autonomic nervous system has learned to take you when you're in need of protection, start by first anchoring in the ventral state. This is where you feel safe, your system is regulated, and your patterns of connection are found. Try placing a hand on your body where you feel the energy of your ventral home. Settle here for a moment and feel the safety and regulation that is present.

And now let your system show you your home away from home, the place where you go to find protection when the safety of connection is lost. Remember, you're still safe in your ventral home; you're going on a journey while staying safely anchored here. You're bringing gratitude for the ways this home away from home has sheltered you along with curiosity and a wish to learn more about this place.

Invite this place that has rescued you when the world has felt too dangerous to show you the ways it works in service of your survival. Invite information through images and words. Just listen and take things in without any thought that you need to change anything. Stay open to learning, to hearing, to understanding the protective intentions of this place.

Take a moment to send a message of gratitude to this state, this home away from home that's been such an important part of your life. You know this place now in a new way, can journey here again when you want, and can trust that your home away from home will be welcoming in the moments when your system reaches for protection. Now, return to present time. Come back to this time and this place. Take a moment to reflect on the journey you just took. Document what you discovered and want to remember.

As we reach the end of this chapter, I want to reflect on the ways we are all at times in our lives taken out of connection into protection. We encounter experiences that are too much for our capacity to stay anchored in ventral safety and connection, and our old, familiar patterns of sympathetic fight and flight or dorsal collapse come to the rescue. Sometimes it's a fleeting event that sparks a moment of protection, and sometimes we find ourselves in situations with the ongoing potential to take us out of connection into protection. None of us can stay permanently engaged with the world and the people around us from our patterns of connection. It is an unreasonable, and unattainable, expectation of ourselves and others. In fact, it is our ability to recognize when we move into a place of protection and find our way back into connection that is the hallmark of resilience.

We are works in progress, and our autonomic nervous systems are listening and learning in each moment. Our ability to connect with awareness to our autonomic experiences naturally ebbs and flows. My work, and your work, is to notice the move into protection, bring awareness to it, stay out of self-judgment, and bring some self-compassion so that we can return to our anchor in safety and connection. Some days finding my way out of protection feels beyond my reach, and other days I'm able to easily find my way to back to my anchor in connection. My invitation to you is to notice your patterns, bring self-compassion to your experiences of protection, and take delight in your times of connection.

7

Anchoring in Safety

In the middle of winter, I at last discovered that
there was in me an invincible summer.

ALBERT CAMUS

I think of our ventral vagal state of regulation as the autonomic
nervous system's invincible summer. It is an embodied, biological
resource that is always present, available, and there to guide us toward
well-being. Although circumstances may make us feel disconnected
from this resource, we all have a ventral vagal state that we can reconnect with and use to anchor in safety.

Ventral vagal, at the top of the hierarchy, is the essential ingredient for our well-being. While one autonomic state is not better
than another and each has a nonreactive, everyday role along with
its survival role, it's the energy of ventral that we need to be in active
connection with in order to feel safe and to engage with the world.
When our ventral vagal state is enlivened and overseeing the system,
our sympathetic and dorsal vagal states work in the background, helping us stay physically and psychologically healthy. When the ventral
state is no longer in charge, we miss its regulating influence and experience health challenges, feel distress in relationships, and have difficulty
navigating our daily lives. Without our anchor in the ventral system,
we are at sea, lost and confused.

Whether fully anchored in ventral, or just having a toehold there,
when we feel enough of this energy of safety, we have access to our four

pathways of connection and are able to meet the challenges in our day. Rather than thinking we need to be fully immersed we can think about having a critical mass of ventral. We only need enough of a connection to ventral to bring the system online and keep it operational.

There are times when I feel in danger of being overwhelmed by the demands of my day. When that happens, I remind myself that although I may not feel deeply rooted in regulation, I can hold on to just enough ventral energy to stay organized and engaged and manage to make it through my day. I imagine reaching for ventral connection. Sometimes I use the image of reaching for ventral and other times I actually stretch my arm up over my head to reach for some regulating energy. Then I begin to hear the ventral story that reassures me there is in fact enough regulating energy available in my system and I can stay in connection with it. What is your image of connecting with enough ventral to make it safely through your day? Experiment with seeing the image in your imagination and bringing it to life through an action.

Concentric Circles

One way to explore the energies and actions of the nervous system is through the imagery of three circles.

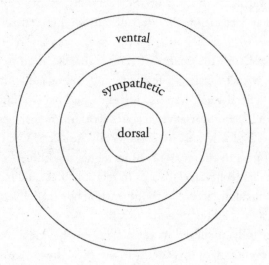

Image 7.1 Three circles of the autonomic nervous system

Imagine the dorsal vagal system as the first and center circle. This is where the story of the autonomic nervous system begins, both in the evolutionary history of human beings and in our development within the womb. This center circle is surrounded by a larger circle, representing the sympathetic system, and these two circles are held by an outer circle representing our ventral vagal system. This outer circle is the last to come online, developing in the third trimester of pregnancy (around thirty weeks on) and continuing to develop through the first one or two years of life.

The metaphor I use is of the ventral vagal system encircling the sympathetic and dorsal vagal systems, holding them both in a warm embrace. When I want to extend ventral vagal energy to someone, I'll often hold my arms out as if I'm offering a hug and let them know I'm sending them my ventral vagal energy. I do that with clients, with colleagues, and in my trainings, and it's become a shorthand that I use to let people know I'm holding them in the safety and regulation of my ventral vagal energy; I'm offering them a ventral vagal embrace. As you read these words, imagine that my arms are reaching out to offer you my ventral vagal energy. See if you can receive that and take that in.

Now try it yourself. Anchor in ventral and feel the ways your system is in balance. Explore how you can offer your ventral vagal energy to someone else. While outstretched arms work for me, try a variety of movements and find the one that's a fit for your system. Experiment and see the movement that emerges. Once you find your movement, use it to extend your energy to someone. Feel what happens for you when you use your movement to make an offer, and imagine what happens for them as they receive the invitation. Then find someone to experiment with. This can be done either remotely or in person. See how it feels to be with someone and hold them in your ventral embrace. Ask the other person what it's like on their end. Play with changing the movement and see what happens on both ends of the experience. Find the way of connecting that feels co-regulating.

Exploration:
Lighting Up Your Circles

Begin by imagining the principal colors that represent the three circles of your autonomic nervous system. Invite your brain to take a rest and, rather than making a cognitive choice, let your autonomic nervous system be your guide. Start with finding the color of your center dorsal circle. Then add the color of your surrounding sympathetic circle. And finally the color of your ventral outer ring that holds the others in a circle of safety.

Explore hand motions to accompany each circle. I sometimes hold my hands clasped tightly together imagining dorsal, spread my fingers apart, just touching, for sympathetic, and then have my hands wide apart to hold the other two in ventral. Along with hand motions, explore other ways to hold your states. You might imagine holding three different-sized balls of light or three streams of energy. Take a moment and experiment with the variety of ways you can hold your states.

From this starting point, the next step is to get to know the ways your states intertwine. For this we move beyond the basic colors and invite shades of color and the comingling of colors. Begin with the ventral state and see how color fills your circle. There might be a variety of colors that make up this circle or different shades of one color. See how the colors of your ventral vagal system illustrate the qualities of anchoring in safety and connection. Watch your colors change as you feel how this energy shapes the ways you navigate safely through the world.

Now add the shades and colors of your sympathetic circle. See how the colors of your two circles complement each other. Sense into the connection between your ventral and sympathetic systems. Feel the ways your sympathetic system adds energy and your ventral system regulates it.

See how the colors blend and separate. And now add the shades and colors of your inner dorsal circle. What appears to represent the slow and steady energy of this state? Notice the similarities and differences between these colors and the colors in your other two circles.

Travel from circle to circle to move between your states. Watch each circle light up as you travel from one to the next. Each has its own individual color palette and brings import-ant benefits for your well-being. Finish your exploration by seeing your three circles all light up together.

When the ventral circle is actively embracing the other two, we can experience physical and psycholog-ical well-being and all of the emergent properties of a system in regulation. Some of the physical health benefits include reduced incidents of heart dis-ease, regulated blood pressure, a healthy immune system, reduced inflammation, and good digestion. Mental health bene-fits include reduced stress, less depression and anxiety, and increased self-compassion and compassion. See the intertwining of your circles and soak in the qualities that accompany this state of well-being.[1]

> There are many flavors of ventral, but the common ingredient is the neuroception of safety that underlies the state.

The Many Flavors of Ventral

While we often think a ventral state is characterized by being calm or happy, our ventral vagal system actually brings a multitude of experi-ences. Along with calm and happy, when we're anchored in our ventral state, we can be excited, joy filled, aware, engaged, passionate, curious, compassionate, alert, ready, and focused. There are many flavors of ventral, but the common ingredient is the neuroception of safety that underlies the state. Take a moment to see what words describe your ventral vagal experiences.

Exploration:
A Ventral Continuum

Using a continuum is an easy way to get to know our personal ventral flavors. With a continuum, we map the gradual changes that happen between first dipping a toe in the ventral state and being fully immersed in the experience. To create your continuum, start by moving into connection with your ventral vagal system. Find it in your body, bring your landscape to life, or reconnect with your ventral vagal circle. Feel the first stirrings of ventral energy. What would you name this moment? What would you label this place on your continuum? Some examples include ease, softening, relaxing, arriving, or present. Listen to your nervous system and find the word that names this moment for you.

Now imagine the other end of the continuum, the place where you are fully immersed in the abundance of your ventral vagal energy. What is the name of this place? It might be abundance, alive, feeling at one with, or passionate. Listen and let your nervous system send you the word for this place.

Having named the experiences of entering and of being fully immersed in the ventral vagal system, you now can travel along the continuum to find the flavors of ventral safety that are in the space between. You might see your continuum as a line and move along it from one end to the other or imagine traveling around your ventral vagal circle. Or your continuum may appear in a totally new design. Experiment until you find the shape that represents your experience. Draw that shape on paper and add the names for entering and immersion. Slowly move around your continuum, stopping to feel the flavors. Name each of the ventral experiences you find and add them to your continuum.

When you've moved from one end to the other, slowly travel your continuum in both directions. Feel the variety of experiences possible and the changes that happen between dipping a toe in the energy of regulation and being fully anchored in safety. Stop at each point to feel the way that particular flavor of ventral comes alive.

There are a number of ways to use your continuum. Regularly return to your continuum and travel from end to end to deepen your connection to your ventral state. When you feel yourself beginning to be pulled into a state of protection and need to find your way to safety and regulation, go to the entry point on your continuum and find your way to the beginnings of ventral safety and regulation.

Your continuum is a map of safety and regulation that evolves as you get to know your ventral vagal system. Over time, you may find more places you want to name or names you want to change. Whether you draw a simple line and add words or create an artistic representation, your continuum is a resource that helps you strengthen your pathways of connection.

Glimmers

While we may have extended periods of time when we move through the world anchored in safety and connection, we also have micro-moments when we feel a spark of ventral energy. I call these glimmers. Glimmers are all around us, but from a state of protection they are very hard to find. Even when we are anchored in safety and connection, we can miss glimmers if we're not looking.

Humans have a built-in negativity bias. In order to support our survival, we're wired to respond more intensely to negative experiences than equally intense positive ones. We have to actively look for, take notice of, and keep track of these moments, or micro-moments, of safety and connection that are our glimmers. Otherwise they can easily pass right by without our knowing. As we begin to bring awareness to our glimmers, the moments begin to add up. We begin to feel more and more ventral energy and build our capacity to anchor there. Glimmers help us travel an upward spiral of safety and connection, and our foundation of regulation is strengthened.[2]

Finding glimmers doesn't mean that we don't also experience suffering. Rather, it's an acknowledgment that our nervous system is capable of holding both moments of safety and moments of survival. It's easy to forget this when we're immersed in a time of distress, and yet, when we bring an intention to notice glimmers, we feel the response of our nervous system to these moments of ventral vagal energy.

Stop for a moment and look around you. Is there a glimmer waiting to be noticed?

Exploration: Finding Glimmers

Yesterday I spotted a red cardinal and stopped for a moment to watch him. Later in the day I smelled the scent of fresh-cut grass through my window. These glimmers from yesterday make me curious about what I'll find on my path today. This is the commonly reported experience of glimmers. Once we begin to see them, we look for more and discover glimmers are not uncommon experiences. When we are open to finding them, they show up frequently in our daily lives.

Connecting with a Glimmer

How do you know you've connected with a glimmer? You may experience it in your body. One of the ways I recognize a glimmer is with a feeling of softening around my eyes and the beginning of a smile. A thought may catch your attention, or you may notice a glimmer through your senses: a smell, a taste, a sight, a sound, the touch of something. Take a moment to notice how you know you've encountered a glimmer.

A glimmer can be a micro-moment that's predictably present in your world. For me this is seeing the stars in the early morning. I'm an early-morning person, and many mornings when I get up, I go outside and look up at the sky just to stand under the stars and take in that moment. Is there a predictably present glimmer for you to connect with? Glimmers can also be unexpected moments that appear on your path. In the moment when you feel the spark of a flavor of ventral vagal energy, stop, notice, and take it in.

Setting an Intention

Setting an intention is a way to support this new practice. My glimmer intention is to look for the glimmers that are on my path today waiting for me to find them. I have a friend who made an intention to see one glimmer a day for a week and another whose intention was to look for a glimmer to begin her day. Take a moment and create your own glimmer intention. Write your intention and then read it out loud to yourself. Does your intention feel doable? Set an intention that feels anchored in a ventral vagal sense of possibility. An intention can feel too small to catch your interest or too big to use successfully. Play with the words until you find the ones that are just right for your nervous system to say yes to.

When we make an intention to look for glimmers, we're often surprised by what we find. Glimmers are all around us as we move through our daily activities. They are drops of ventral energy that bring nourishing moments of connection. Our challenge is to notice them when they happen. It's helpful to keep a record of glimmers to track the many places and ways they appear in our lives. When we know where we predictably find glimmers, we can make a practice of returning to those places and experiencing the ventral vagal energy they offer. Keep a glimmer notebook or find a place to note them in your journal.

The Fleeting Nature of a Glimmer

Sometimes, rather than bringing a micro-moment of ventral energy, beginning to find glimmers can feel dangerous. I have a friend who compared her experience of glimmers to building a sandcastle at the surf's edge and having it swept away. For her, the fleeting nature of a glimmer brought sadness. If your experience as you begin to search for and see glimmers is like this, start by looking for a predictable glimmer, something you can count on to appear in your life. My friend's love of nature and daily walks offered her a way to regularly notice a glimmer and make glimmers a predictable and nourishing part of her daily life. Being able to count on glimmers appearing and reappearing on her walks created the safety she needed to be open to the unexpected glimmer moments.

Everyday Safety

Along with glimmers, our everyday experiences offer opportunities to anchor in ventral vagal safety. Often, the simple things we do, things we're intuitively drawn to and our nervous system guides us toward, are regulating for us even without our awareness. And while the act of engaging with these brings our ventral vagal state alive, when we stop and notice the moment, bring it into awareness, and intentionally savor it, we deepen the experience and strengthen the state. When we find easy ways to reach for ventral, we harness the power of these ordinary experiences.

In my conversations with people around the world, it seems that what we choose to wear is a common way we wrap ourselves in ventral vagal energy. We have a favorite shirt, sweater, sweatpants, or shoes, and when we put them on, we feel the safety, warmth, and connection of a ventral vagal experience. I have a favorite sweater I love to wear. It brings me a sense of confidence and at the same time I feel comforted by the memories of other times I've worn my sweater and felt wrapped in ventral regulation. Do you have something like that, something that you put on that makes you feel immediately safe and comforted and ready to meet the world?

Another way to feel anchored in the ventral state is through our sense of smell. Odors have an impact on the autonomic nervous system and smelling a familiar, pleasant odor is a way to anchor in the energy of regulation. I love the smell of the sea and pine trees.

These are the smells of home for me. I light a scented candle and find my way to regulation. Think about your own experience with smell. What are the scents that take you to your ventral home, and how can you bring them into your environment?

There are places in the world that bring our ventral vagal state alive and that we're drawn to explore or inhabit. In certain environments we easily connect to our ventral energy. I feel this in what I call *ends of the earth* places. I love the places where the land meets the sea at the very furthest point, the places that are still a bit wild and isolated. I have a friend who feels the same thing in the midst of a bustling city and another who longs to be within sight of the mountains. We each have our own places where we feel an embodied sense of being home, places where we feel reliably and deeply anchored in safety.

What are the environments that feel like your autonomic home? Where are the places in your world that bring that experience alive?

In addition to the larger environments we're pulled to, we also have personal places where we predictably find a ventral connection. I have a corner in my home where I sit and feel content. A friend shared with me that he has a favorite place in his local coffee shop, and another friend told me his place was sitting under a special tree. Look around your daily living environment and find your personal connection place.

And then there are objects that bring the tangible reminder that we can find our way back to a ventral connection and anchor there. Some of my favorite objects are beach stones. As a child I learned that a stone with a ring around it is a lucky stone. As an adult, I regularly go to the beach near my home and pick up stones, looking for a lucky one. Even harder to find are heart-shaped stones, so I consider it a moment to treasure when I find one of those in my stone search. I have a jar of lucky stones and heart-shaped stones that I've collected on my beach walks. They are on my kitchen windowsill where I see them every day, serving as a tangible reminder of regulation. When I want a bit of a stronger connection to that reminder of regulation, I take a stone from the jar and carry it with me. Take a moment and find something that reminds you of the feeling of being anchored in regulation and then put it somewhere you'll see it as you move through your day.

With this new awareness of some of the elements that bring your ventral vagal state to life and help you feel anchored in safety, now explore ways to bring this awareness into action. You can grab your favorite sweater or T-shirt, have scents around, and savor the moments when you're in places that nurture your system. Place objects around your environment as reminders of your ventral connection and choose something special to carry with you. Take some time to create your own personal plan.

Exploration: SAFE

Like many of us, I like acronyms. They help me remember the elements of a practice. When I was working with ways to anchor in safety, the four elements of **S**tory, **A**ction, **F**eeling, and **E**mbodied sensation became the acronym **SAFE**, with each element being a step in the process of creating a SAFE story. In the following sections you can follow the prompts to write your own SAFE story and read the elements of mine.

Anchor in Regulation

Before beginning the process, find your way to regulation and take a moment to anchor there. You might use your circle imagery and see your outer ventral circle light up, encircling your other states. You might connect with the place in your body where the ventral state comes alive or use one of the elements of everyday safety you just discovered.

S - Story

Choose a story for your SAFE exploration that holds a flavor of safety that you'd like to revisit and rewrite. Bring it alive with the parts that are important to you. Some stories of safety are held in memories while others are happening in present-time experiences. Choose a moment you're interested in exploring and expanding into a larger story of safety. Write about the moment. Describe the details that are meaningful to you.

My story: *Recently I have been feeling some of the challenges of aging. I've discovered this can easily bring worry or a sense of sorrow, and I need ways to feel anchored in safety. My story is from a memory of climbing a tree in the backyard of my childhood home. The tree had boards nailed to the trunk, making it easy to climb high up into a canopy of branches. I made many childhood memories in this tree, and now I imagine that the tree and I are growing old together. The shape of the tree limbs, many of them twisted over time, shows how this tree has survived. My limbs, twisted in their own ways, tell my survival story.*

A - Action

Move to the element of action and see what happens in this story. Write about what you do here that's important for you to remember.

My story: *I imagine I'm standing in the shadow of the tree, finding sanctuary from the bright light of the sun. Then I imagine sitting with my back against the sturdy trunk. I remember all the times I climbed high up in the tree and looked out at the world with delight.*

F - Feeling

Look at your feelings. When this story of safety is alive in your system, what are some of the feelings that come along with that? Write about the feelings you remember of what happened in the story and the feelings that come from writing the story now.

My story: *I remember the joy of being a kid with a tree to climb and the feeling of freedom I felt when I was high up in my tree. I feel a bit of sadness that I can no longer climb the way I did when I was young but still feel the sense of freedom and joy in* *my life. Then I think about the roots of my tree and the way these roots support health and growth, and I feel the safety of being deeply rooted in my life. I feel the combination of being free and rooted, and I discover I'm content.*

E - Embodied Sensation

End with your embodied sensations. How do you feel this story of safety in your body? Write about the sensations you remember and how revisiting the story is felt in your body now.

My story: *My body remembers the excitement of climbing and the feeling of energy in my hands and feet. I feel that same excitement flowing easily in my body now. As I remember my connection with my tree, I can feel my energy moving up to the sky as I climb and down to the earth as I feel the strength of the tree's roots.*

When you finish writing your story, give it a title, read it again, and feel how you can anchor in your story of safety. Over time, write a few SAFE stories. Many people find writing SAFE stories helps them reconnect to remembered moments of safety and bring the experience alive in the present. See if this way of connecting with ventral safety and regulation fits for you.

Many Ways to Celebrate Safety

As we find our way to ventral safety more often and with more ease, we want to find ways to stay there, soak in the experience, and get the physical and psychological benefits of a system that's anchored in that regulating energy. When we live with an autonomic nervous system that gets pulled out of the ventral space and can't find its way back, some of the ways we suffer are with depression, anxiety, digestive problems, respiratory problems, chronic fatigue, social isolation, and loneliness. The benefits of a system that can flexibly return to the ventral state include a sense of subjective well-being, an increased capacity for friendship, and the ability for self-compassion and compassion for others.[3]

We find our way to an anchor in the ventral space on our own and with others. No matter how we arrive, it's important to notice the return and appreciate the process. Appreciation can take many forms. It may be a quiet expression of gratitude, taking the opportunity to savor, or a simple acknowledgment of the moment. And sometimes we want to mark the moment in a big, energy-filled way. While there is no one way to notice and appreciate, the important part of the process is to be aware of finding our way back to the ventral state and acknowledging that return in the way that feels right in that moment.

A friend shared with me her experience of doing just that. Her home away from home is what she calls her place of dorsal deadness. She is familiar with the experience of going there and eventually finding her way back to ventral safety. While she was accustomed to making that journey, she wanted to find a way to recognize her ability to come back to ventral security and hold on to the experience. We had talked about the benefits of acknowledging the return to being anchored in regulation and some of the ways to do that. Here is what she shared with me:

> I felt the first stirring of energy in my body that signals I am beginning to come back to life, and I turned toward it. Next I felt a bit of hope returning and that opened up my well-traveled path back to ventral and feeling alive again. I experimented with ways to honor and deepen this experience so I could stay anchored there. What I discovered was that feeling grateful for finding my way to safety and regulation was not enough. I needed a more active celebration to bring my system alive. It was the act of celebrating by saying out loud and with passion, "I've arrived! I'm here!" that helped me feel fully alive and anchored again. I've discovered that for my system, actively acknowledging by celebrating out loud is an important part of the experience. When I celebrate, I strengthen my ability to stay anchored in safety.

See if celebrating resonates for you. Imagine being pulled into a state of protection, finding your way back to ventral safety, and celebrating the return to regulation. Try some phrases on for size. It may be that your system doesn't want this kind of acknowledgment, or like my friend, you may find this is a practice that helps make your return to and anchoring in ventral security much easier.

We also find our way back to safety in connection with others and with a quieter recognition of the experience. We can use moments of co-regulation to reduce experiences of mobilization or shutdown and strengthen our capacity to stay anchored in safety. I have a friend who is used to getting pulled into a mobilized flight response and getting stuck there. That experience takes her out of connection with the people around her. When she is mobilized, she feels like everyone is against her and the only choice is to run. Here is her story of connecting with a friend and finding a change in her ability to stay anchored in safety:

> Even though I was with a good friend, I still felt the pull
> of mobilization and the need to escape. Later I could look
> back and see that although I was pulled into a survival
> state, my friend never stopped being my friend. She
> was always on my side. At the time I couldn't see that.
> My biology wouldn't let me sense that or believe it. So
> I asked my friend to help me create a statement that I
> could read aloud or say to myself when I was anchored
> in safety and another statement to use when I began to
> feel the need to escape. From my anchor in safety my
> statement was, "I'm here and can take in the joy of being
> with others," and in the beginning pull toward flight
> my statement was, "If I need to run away from danger,
> I have a friend who will go with me." What I discovered
> is that after a few weeks of using these two simple
> statements, I'm less apt to feel the intense need to escape,
> and I'm much more able to stay anchored in safety.

See if this way of noticing your return to ventral security and anchoring there resonates for you. Think about someone who you would want to use as a co-regulating resource. What statements could you write to use that connection to anchor in safety? Your system may find this useful or you may find that co-regulation is not your preferred pathway.

Savoring

The practice of savoring helps us make the most of a moment, or a micro-moment, of safety and regulation. Savoring is about seeing and celebrating the little things in everyday life. We savor when we recognize an experience in the moment, when we remember a moment and reminisce, and when we anticipate an upcoming experience. When we bring these moments into awareness and spend just a short amount of time actively engaged in attending to them, the benefits are both immediate, as we feel anchored in ventral safety, and longer term, with gains in physical and emotional well-being. Our immune systems are strengthened, and we feel more creative, identify more life satisfaction, are more resilient, and have a reduced risk of depression. Rather than singular moments, micro-moments of savoring accumulate. With a savoring practice, they add up and shape our systems toward connection.[4]

Exploration:
Attend, Appreciate, Amplify

Our autonomic nervous systems inherently know the way back home to safety and regulation, and we each develop our own ways to deepen that experience. One of the ways we can connect to our ventral state and anchor there is through the process of savoring. When we savor, we attend, appreciate, and amplify a ventral experience. Savoring is a brief, three-step, twenty- to thirty-second practice that easily fits into the flow of a day:

1. First, attend. Bring a ventral vagal moment into awareness and stop to notice it.

2. Next, appreciate the moment. Stay with your awareness.

3. Finally, amplify. Hold the moment in focused awareness for twenty to thirty seconds. Feel the fullness of the moment.

Savoring is a practice of twenty to thirty seconds at the most, making it possible to do many times during the course of the day. Experiment with this. Think of a moment, or even a micro-moment, when you felt connected to the energy of your ventral vagal system. Simply be with that experience. Feel the ways your body brings you the ventral vagal energy and the ways the experience comes to life. Spend about twenty seconds there and then come back to the present moment.

You may find it easy to savor your experience for twenty seconds, and in that case, you could extend your appreciation to thirty seconds. Or you may find it challenging and feel a move from amplifying into what's called a dampening experience that happens when thoughts interrupt the process and stop the savoring. We may find ourselves thinking we don't deserve to feel this, it's dangerous to feel good, or something bad will happen if we stop and appreciate the moment. This is not an uncommon experience when we begin to explore ways to attend and appreciate. When this happens, start slowly with five or ten seconds and build toward twenty or thirty. Find the amount of time that supports your ability to attend, appreciate, and amplify. Whenever the practice moves from an experience of deepening to one of dampening, stop. Be gentle, be patient, be persistent. Over time you'll find your capacity to savor will increase.

Share and Deepen

We savor again when we add language to the experience in order to share it with someone. Remember, our nervous system longs for connection, and sharing our savoring story with someone deepens the experience. Find someone who will meet you with an open heart and a readiness to listen. Your savoring comes alive in the retelling, and the person you are sharing with often feels as if they are joining you in the ventral vagal–inspired moment.

As we reach the end of this chapter of exploring ways to anchor in safety, I want to leave you with this line from a Rumi poem: "There's a candle in your heart ready to be kindled." I think our ventral vagal state, along with the energies it brings alive, is a candle that is always lit, and when nourished and cherished it will burn brighter and warmer, bringing us health, growth, and restoration.

8

Gentle Shaping

Everything is accomplished bit by bit.

CHARLES BAUDELAIRE,
MY HEART LAID BARE AND OTHER PROSE WRITINGS

With an understanding of the ways our autonomic nervous systems work and the beginning ability to befriend them, we turn our attention to gently shaping our systems in new ways. The autonomic nervous system guides us as we move through the world. Without awareness, our patterns simply work in the background. Even when our patterns are regulating and bring well-being, if we don't turn toward them and actively engage with them, we don't benefit in the deepest way possible. With attention and intention, we can shape our system in ways that resource the pathways that nourish our well-being.

Our pathways often take us into what is known in biology as a positive feedback loop. In this context, the word *positive* simply means that the pattern continues to be active. A positive feedback loop can create an upward spiral of connection. It might begin with a glimmer that brings a moment of relaxation in your body followed by a joyful thought that then creates a readiness for seeing the next glimmer. We want to recognize and resource this kind of positive feedback loop.

A positive feedback loop can also keep us caught in a cycle of protection. Our survival states are accompanied by self-criticism and self-blame, and those messages reinforce the survival pattern. Even a brief experience of a protective loop exerts a powerful pull and without interrupting the pattern, we can't reshape our systems. For example, a story I often find myself pulled into is that I'm a misfit, I don't belong here, I don't have the right to be here. This comes from a dorsal vagal place of disconnection, and once I start hearing those stories, the gravitational pull gets stronger. It becomes harder to find my way to ventral regulation or even remember that it is a possibility.

Take some time to explore your own loops. Start by looking at a moment of mobilization. Feel your embodied response and then hear the thought that starts this particular survival story. Watch how your thoughts and stories get stronger and begin to magnify the experience. Continue by looking at a loop that ends in collapse. Notice your embodied response, listen to how this story begins, and feel how you are pulled into the experience, falling deeper into disconnection. Complete the exploration by looking at a loop that creates an upward spiral of connection. Notice the embodied response. Feel how ventral connection is alive and active in your system and takes you into a loop that brings well-being. Follow the thoughts that anchor you in your story of safety.

Stretch, Don't Stress

It's with an attitude of friendship and an intention to befriend that we can engage with our systems to shape new patterns and deepen ones that are already working. Our goal in shaping new patterns is to stretch but not stress our system. We want to stretch, feel the shape of a new pattern, and spend a moment savoring it. When we feel as if we need to power through an experience or that we need to suffer to see results, we stress the system and move into one of the survival states. Once that happens, we're no longer shaping. Instead, we're held in a familiar pattern of protection. The "no pain, no gain" model doesn't work with autonomic reshaping. In order to change, it's necessary to find the right degree of challenge that keeps us safely anchored in the shaping process.

Shaping is about attending moment to moment to what is happening in our autonomic nervous system, connecting with the information, and respecting what we find. Both the excitement and the challenge of shaping our systems is that we never quite know where we're heading. What works today may be too much or not enough tomorrow. We're going on an autonomic adventure, and we need to take enough ventral regulation with us to be safe on the journey. It's when we ignore our nervous system and instead travel the path our brains want us to follow that we move from stretching and shaping into stress and survival.

I've learned through my own experiences not to ignore my nervous system. My brain may have an idea about what to do, but regardless of what my brain decides, my nervous system is going to

> When we feel as if we need to power through an experience or that we need to suffer to see results, we stress the system and move into one of the survival states.

take the action it deems necessary to ensure my survival. Recently, I planned to enjoy a slow start to the day. I had every intention of taking my time and not rushing into my workday, but the mobilizing energy of my sympathetic nervous system was too strong, and my intention to take it slow and ease into the day was gone. I began to hear my self-critical voices, and I had to work hard not to be pulled into a familiar story of shame and self-blame. When I turned toward my autonomic nervous system, I could appreciate that this morning my nervous system had other ideas.

Once I came into connection from a place of respect and curiosity, I was able to hear what was underneath this survival response. My sympathetic system was pushing me to get going out of a fear that if I didn't, I'd fall behind in my work and never meet my deadlines. That fear quickly led to a story about being a failure. Knowing the story that was fueling the response gave me the information I needed to adjust my plan for the morning so I could use the mobilizing energy to be productive but not driven. I got out my to-do list and wrote "this week" at the top to remind myself I had time. Not wanting to dive headlong into work and at the same time needing to respect the need to take action, I sat in a favorite spot with my morning coffee and spent time organizing a plan to make my way through the items on my to-do list over the coming week. Although it wasn't the lazy morning I had planned, I was able to partner with my nervous system, and rather than simply getting up and going to work, I could make time to reflect and move through the start of my day with some ease.

Try that for yourself now. Think about a time recently when you had an idea about how something was going to go and what you had intended wasn't what happened. Feel the flavor of survival response that got in the way. How did your nervous system try and get your attention? Notice what it was like for your brain and your nervous system to not be on the same page. Notice how you felt that internal battle. And then imagine turning toward the response that was getting in the way of what you had planned and listening to the story that your nervous system wanted you to hear. What was fueling the behaviors and thoughts? As you hear that story, see how your experience changes.

An essential step in the shaping process is to know when you've moved beyond stretching into stressing, beyond a place where you're engaged with your patterns to a place where you've been hijacked by a pattern and pulled into survival. I've come to know I'm losing my ventral anchor when my thoughts begin to get just a bit chaotic or disorganized. I start to feel stuck in one story and forget that there are other possibilities.

The stretch-to-stress continuum is a good way to recognize the signs that let you know you're stretching and shaping and the ones that let you know when you begin to cross the line into the danger zone of stress and survival.

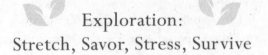

Exploration:
Stretch, Savor, Stress, Survive

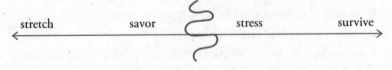

Image 8.1 Stretch-to-stress continuum

Draw a line on paper and along it evenly space out the words *stretch*, *savor*, *stress*, and *survive*. The midpoint on the line should be the place between savor and stress so that stretch and savor are on one side and stress and survive are on the other. Mark that point in a way that draws your attention. Up to that midpoint is ventral space; beyond the midpoint is sympathetic and dorsal. Give your line the colors, textures, length, and width that you want. Many people find adding images helps them deepen their connection. On my continuum I have the picture of a kite flying at the end of a long string for stretch, a nautilus shell for savor, a jagged heart shape for stress, and a hollow-eyed emoji representing my home away from home in the dorsal state for survive. See what images go along with the words on your continuum.

In this exploration we're going to use fingers to "walk the line," but you can also create a line in space and actually walk along it. Place both fingers on the spot that marks the midpoint on the line and remember a time when you felt balanced just at the point of change. Give this place a name. My name for this place is "the edge." Invite your autonomic nervous system to send you a word. Play with the words until you find the ones that feel just right to mark this place of change from shaping to surviving. Now place one finger on either side of that point—one finger on the stretch and savor side and one on the stress and survive side. Feel the different energies in each place. Shift the balance between your fingers and feel what happens to your sense of being anchored in ventral safety.

Now go to the beginning of the line, to the place marked "stretch." Feel what it's like in that spot where you're ready to shape your system in some small new way. Feel how your autonomic nervous system lets you know it is supporting you in this process, on board with making a change. Now move your fingers to the spot marked "savor." Remember what it feels like to stop and take in a change, to notice fully, perhaps even to celebrate.

Move between these two points to take in the ways a small stretch and a moment to savor support shaping. When you are ready, move to the midpoint again and stop for a moment before moving to the other side of the continuum. Remind yourself that this exploration is about information gathering.

We are now going to make a fact-finding trip to the territory of stress and survive. In this exploration we don't want to fully embody those states, we want to just get a flavor of them. Move your fingers to the mark labeled "stress" and get to know the flavors of this experience. How does your nervous system let you know you've crossed the midpoint and you're no longer in a shaping practice?

And now make the last move to the survival mark. Stay there just long enough to take in the ways your sympathetic and dorsal vagal states bring an adaptive survival response. Feel how in this place you are now reinforcing patterns of protection. Move back to stress and notice the difference. What happens when you take the step back from survival to stress?

Then return to the midpoint, tracking your nervous system shifts and the thoughts that emerge. Move to the regulated side of the line and find your way back to stretch. Reflect on the experience of creating your continuum and moving between the points. Take time to document what you discovered and what you feel is important to remember.

There are a variety of ways to use your continuum. When you feel you've crossed over the midpoint into a moment of stress, use your continuum to find your way back to the stretch side. If you find yourself all the way at the end of the line in a survival response, use your continuum to reduce the response, return to stress, and then take the step back to midpoint. From the midpoint you can reflect on what made the experience too challenging for you in that moment. When you are working with a new experience, use your continuum to stay on the stretch and savor side. When you want to explore the edges of a new experience, stand on the midpoint and feel the moment when you move into stress. "Walk" between stretch and savor to deepen new pathways.

Nourishing or Depleting

There are two pathways to follow in reshaping our systems. One is to recognize patterns that are driven by mobilization and disconnection, notice the patterns that are draining, and work to reduce or resolve them. The other is to recognize patterns that are nourishing and find ways to replicate, deepen, and experience more of them. We are naturally drawn toward the patterns that are draining as we feel the effects in physical symptoms and emotional distress. Attending to changing these patterns is often where we begin but can't be where we end. In order to fully experience well-being, we need to attend not only to the pathways that drain but also to the ones that fill.

The first step is the ability to recognize how we experience moments as draining or filling. From there we can move on to reducing or resolving the experiences that are draining and replicating the ones that are filling. Using the building blocks of the hierarchy, start at the bottom in the dorsal state with an experience that's autonomically draining. When I feel the pull of my dorsal system, I notice a slight numbing in my body, I take a step back from my environment, and I begin to think that I don't belong. Reflect on a recent experience that led you into a dorsal collapse and notice what happens in your body. What are your behaviors and beliefs in this dorsal place of autonomic draining? As you begin to recognize what happens for you, take a moment to document what you find.

Move up one place on the hierarchy and think about an experience that brought you into the mobilization of your sympathetic fight and flight response. In this place, I feel a jolt in my upper arms and a tightening in my gut. I can't stay still and begin to feel an intense need to get away. Notice how you feel this draining pattern in your body, your behaviors, and your beliefs. As you recognize what happens here, take a moment to document what you find.

When we arrive at the top of the hierarchy in safety and regulation, the experience changes from draining to filling. When this happens, I feel a sense of ease in my body, I move easily through the day, and I think the world is offering me opportunities to explore. Think about a moment that brings you an experience of ventral vagal resourcing. Notice what happens for you. How does a filling experience show up in your body, your behaviors, and your beliefs? As you begin to recognize what happens for you, document what you find.

With the ability to identify something as draining or filling, you now have a guide to explore your experiences. Using your guide, do a quick survey. Reflect on a few recent experiences and name ones that drained you with an overwhelming need to fight or flee and ones that drained you through numbing and collapse. Then name experiences that nourished you and felt filling.

Shaping our systems in new ways is a gentle process that unfolds over time. While we want change to happen now, in an instant, the autonomic nervous system most often finds its way both to creating new patterns and into deepening the pathways that are already present and nourishing by doing small things over and over. Marie Curie in her *Autobiographical Notes* wrote, "I was taught that the way of progress is neither swift nor easy." Likewise shaping happens not in a flash with one big action but in little moments that add up. Shaping requires us to be patient, to be persistent, and to persevere. The next sections and explorations in this chapter honor this need.

States and Statements

I'm reminded here of Hank Williams's song, "I'm So Lonesome I Could Cry," which lends itself well to this next exercise. We often have a thought that follows the sentence structure, "I'm so _____ [some feeling], I could _____ [some action]." For example, "I'm so tired, I could give up." "I'm so angry, I could scream." "I'm so happy, I could smile at the world." With these kinds of sentences, each autonomic state is sending us a message.

Exploration:
I'm so . . . I could . . .

Begin this exploration by listening in to see what your system is saying. Use the sentence structure "I'm so _____, I could _____" to notice this moment in time and fill in the blanks with whatever words appear.

Reflect on your sentence and see which state was sending you a message. Did the sentence emerge from a ventral state where the words feel regulated, interesting, and filling? Did your words come from your sympathetic state, bringing a flavor of danger and a feeling of being fueled by too much energy? Or maybe the words emerged from your dorsal state and captured the sense of losing hope, disconnecting, and shutting down.

The next step is to write three sentences, one from each of your states. Start by connecting with your dorsal and sympathetic survival states. See what feelings and actions emerge to complete those sentences. End with the feeling and action that creates a ventral-inspired sentence.

Using the sentences you now have for each state, we can explore shaping new patterns by taking the original sentences and writing companion statements for each, keeping the feeling (I'm so) but changing the action (I could). The goal is to bring enough regulating energy to the writing to soften the two survival pathways and deepen the pathway of safety and connection.

Using the examples above, the sentence that emerges from a dorsal state of collapse, "I'm so tired, I could give up," could be changed to, "I'm so tired, I could rest for a bit."

The sentence that is fueled by sympathetic activation, "I'm so angry, I could scream," might become "I'm so angry, I could take a break and come back in a while."

And the original ventral-inspired sentence "I'm so happy, I could smile at the world" could be rewritten as "I'm so happy, I could reach out and spend time with my friends."

Return to your three sentences and the feeling you identified in your dorsal, sympathetic, and ventral sentences (I'm so) and consider a different response (I could). Bring in just a bit of ventral regulating energy to the sentences that were written from your sympathetic and dorsal states and write new endings. To support this you might return to your ventral outer circle and imagine it lighting up, see the ventral vagal landscape you created in your mind's eye, or make contact with the place in your body that connects you with your ventral vagal state. When you feel like you have enough of an anchor in the ventral system to explore a different ending, fill in the action part of those sentences. Use words that gently shape the survival response by adding an action that is guided by the regulation of your ventral system. End your exploration with the sentence you wrote from an anchor in ventral regulation. Add an action that expands the experience and invites you into a moment of savoring.

This is a quick and easy way to look at a pattern and begin to shape it in a new way. We often hear ourselves saying, "I'm so _____, I could _____." As you hear yourself saying this, take that moment to turn toward the first part of the sentence, bring a bit of ventral energy, and look for a different ending.

Breathing into Regulation

Another way to shape our system is with breath. Breath is controlled by the autonomic nervous system. It's an automatic process, but one we can also intentionally manipulate. Breath is a direct pathway to our autonomic nervous system, making it both a regulating resource and an activator of our survival states. Pranayama (breath practice) has been a part of yoga practices for centuries, and there are many wonderful resources to support you in a deep exploration of the power of breath.

As we explore using breath to shape our systems, it is important to remember that we each breathe in our way. For many of us, breath practices can be a cue of danger. Changing the rhythms and cycles of breathing can quickly begin to shift our autonomic state. Even the act of simply noticing the breath slows and deepens it a bit. As we begin to breathe just a bit slower or take a slightly deeper breath, instead of finding the way to safety and regulation, we may drop into disconnection and collapse.

The normal breathing rate for adults is between twelve and twenty breaths per minute. An easy way to find your breath rate is by counting your exhalations over the course of a minute. This gives you a baseline number to work with as you begin to explore breathing in a different way. In general when we look at breath patterns, longer exhalations (bubble blowing is a playful way to practice long, slow exhalations), slower breathing (use your breath-per-minute rate to track), and resistance breathing (you can get a feel for this by imagining you are blowing air through a straw as you exhale) bring more ventral vagal energy. Rapid breathing, irregular breathing, or sharp inhalations or exhalations increases sympathetic activity, while matching the length of inhalation and exhalation maintains a state of autonomic balance.[1]

Before we move into explorations, let's begin by simply noticing. Find a place on your body where you can feel your breath moving. This might be in your chest, your abdomen, your side ribs, your lower back, or beneath your nostrils. Take time to locate the place where you come into connection with your breath. Follow the pathway of your inhalation and exhalation for a few breath cycles to get to know it.

As you breathe, bring awareness to your vagal brake and how it works. Remember the slight relaxation of your vagal brake and increase in heart rate that happens on the inhale and the reengagement of your vagal brake and decrease in heart rate that accompanies each exhale. Follow a few more breath cycles without changing anything. Simply be with your breath. Now take a moment to get to know the ways your breath and your state are linked. Travel the hierarchy and feel how your breath rhythm changes. Notice how you breathe when you are pulled into a dorsal state of collapse, when you feel the mobilization of a sympathetic fight and flight response, and when you are anchored in ventral safety and regulation.

In the next exercises, we will explore some simple ways to be with your breath and begin to use breath to shape your pathways to regulation. As you explore these practices, let your autonomic nervous system be your guide. Stay anchored in a ventral state and stay on the stretch and savor side of the continuum.

Exploration: Breath Rhythms

One way to bring attention and intention to your breath rhythms is to bring breath and language together by adding words to accompany each inhalation and exhalation. Look for pairs of words that speak to the slight rise of energy that goes along with an inhalation and the return to ease that accompanies the exhalation. For example, *energize* and *rest* or *reach out* and *tune in*. Experiment until you find the combinations of words that fit for you. You may find that one combination feels like a natural fit and want to rely on those words as your connection to breath. Or you may like having a choice and want to find several pairs of words that attune with your breath. Once you have found your words, experiment with using them to bring focused awareness to your breath rhythm. Bring your words to mind as each breath arrives and leaves, and notice what happens. See what happens if you say your words out loud. Try placing your hand on your body where you found your breath in the earlier exploration and see how that changes your experience.

While it's comforting to have sets of words that reliably bring us into connection with our breath, there are also times when we want to experiment to see what words emerge in the moment. Tune in and listen to the words that arrive with your inhalations and the words that accompany your exhalations. Listen for several breath cycles to see if there is a pattern that emerges or if each breath cycle brings a new combination of words. When we stay open and curious, we often discover something new.

Movement accompanies every breath. Our lungs fill and empty, the diaphragm changes shape first to make room for air and then to help push it out, and our chest and abdomen rise and fall. In addition to these biological movements that are tied to our breath rhythms, we can add intentional movement to our inhalations and exhalations and feel our breath moving in ways that bring regulation.

Exploration:
Moving with Breath

As you explore adding movement, you can either imagine moving or express the movement in an action. Either choice will bring the exploration alive, so choose the way that keeps you on the stretch side of the continuum. Begin by inviting a movement to emerge as you inhale. Next explore a movement that accompanies your exhalation. And now join your two movements with your breath cycle and feel your body and breath moving together.

Another way to use breath as a shaping practice is through sighing. Sighing is a natural way our lungs stay healthy. We sigh spontaneously many times an hour, taking a deeper breath to inflate the millions of air sacs in our lungs and then exhaling deeply. Sighing has been called a resetter of our systems, as the long audible exhalation that is the hallmark of a sigh has been shown to directly impact not only our physiology but also our thoughts. In addition to our spontaneous sighs working in the background to bring moments of regulation, we can use intentional sighing as a way to interrupt our state and find a momentary reset and also to deepen an experience of regulation and connection.[2]

Exploration:
Sighing

Begin to notice your breath, not changing it in any way but simply following it. Notice it entering your body, filling your body in its own way, and leaving again. Feel the rhythm of your breath cycle. Now interrupt your breath pattern by inhaling more deeply on the next breath and turning the exhalation into a sigh. Move through a few breath cycles, adding a sigh every now and then.

There are some basic ways we sigh. We sigh with frustration to release some energy, and we sigh when we feel down or depressed in an attempt to bring in some energy. We sigh in relief as we find our way back to regulation and then breathe a sigh of contentment to savor the experience of being safely anchored there.

Explore each way of sighing and feel your response. Start with a sigh of despair. Feel the beginning pull of collapse and the draining of energy that comes with that. Turn your next exhalation into a deep sigh and see what happens as you interrupt the breath pattern. Next let in some of the energy of fight and flight that comes from your sympathetic nervous system. Feel a bit of dysregulation and breathe a sigh of frustration. Let your sigh release some of that mobilizing energy. Notice the thoughts that come along with that sigh and see how your state shifts. Now feel a bit of dysregulation and find your way back to your anchor in regulation. Breathe a sigh of relief and notice the thoughts that come accompany that experience. And as you are held in that place of connection, breathe a sigh of contentment. Let your breath tell the story of ease, of equanimity, of feeling nourished and filled. Listen to the story, take it in, and savor it. The intentional use of sighing is a gentle way of actively shaping the autonomic nervous system.

Feeling Touched

Touch is a basic way the nervous system communicates. When we offer someone a touch, we are sharing the state of our nervous system with them, and when we're touched by someone else, we know the state of their system. Touch can quickly bring us into connection or activate our pathways of protection. Whether it's an intimate touch, a social touch, or a warm, friendly touch, touch is an essential ingredient in well-being. Touch stimulates the autonomic nervous system, supporting reduced depression, anxiety, and stress. Touch calms our cardiovascular system, increases immune function, and reduces pain. Dacher Keltner of the Greater Good Science Center at UC Berkeley has called touch preventative medicine. Even our language reflects the importance we place on touch. We invite people to stay in touch, wonder why people are so touchy, and are touched by experiences.[3]

Exploration: A Touch Continuum

When we miss being touched, we become touch hungry, and with enough moments of touch we are nourished and become touch filled. We regularly travel between these two ends of our touch experience and can return to the use of a continuum to find the stops along the way.

Draw a line, and above the line, mark one end "touch hungry" and the other "touch filled." Find your own labels for those opposite ends and write those below the line. Find the midpoint where you feel the beginning of the shift from hungry to filled and name that place. Then move from that place in either direction and name several points along the way. Feel what happens in your nervous system as you move toward feeling touch filled or touch hungry.

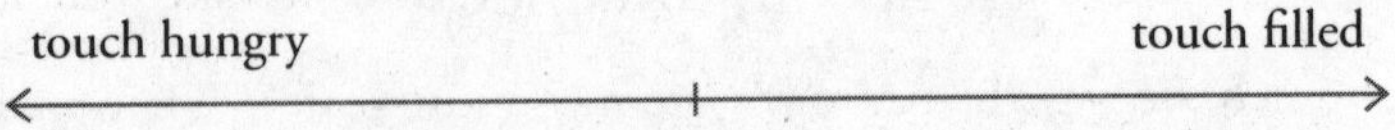

touch hungry   touch filled

←————————————————————|————————————————————→

Image 8.2 Touch continuum

With your personal touch continuum, you can now bring curiosity to where you are on that line. Take a moment to move along your continuum until you find the place that represents your present experience. Knowing where you are gives you the information needed to consider what to do.

If you're on the midpoint, the next choices you make around touch will move you toward feeling hungry or feeling filled. If you're on the hungry side of the line, explore ways to find the moments of touch your system is missing. If you're on the filled side, first see if you are in the place that fits your needs in the moment. If yes, stop and savor that. If you still feel a longing, look for more moments of touch that move you further in the direction of feeling filled.

Our touch memories are held in our nervous system, and when we make contact with a memory we move again into a pattern of protection or connection. Memories of moments when touch was offered in a way that was unexpected or unwanted activate our survival states. Think of times in your life when touch was not welcome and notice when you went to fight and flight and when you went to collapse.

Touch can also bring a regulating response and help us anchor in connection. Look for memories of moments when touch was welcomed and feel how those experiences brought you into safety and connection. Just as our autonomic patterns can be shaped in new ways, research now tells us that we can remember more than one touch and make new touch memories.[4]

If you have someone in your life who you feel safe to explore touch with, you can explore the ways of touching and being touched that bring your ventral vagal state to life and activate your survival states. Does being offered a hand invite your social engagement system to respond with a move toward connection or does it take you into protection? Does a hand on your back bring regulation or activate a survival response? Identify the touches that are disconnecting and look for the ways of touching and being touched that bring you home to ventral regulation and help you anchor there.

Self-touch is another way we commonly experience touch. We put a hand on our forehead when we're feeling overwhelmed. When we're surprised or startled, a natural gesture is the quick intake of breath and a hand over the heart. We put a hand over our heart when we're feeling touched by something special. For many of us, putting a hand on our heart invites a return to regulation and keeping our hand there deepens the experience. Try that now. Place a hand over your heart and feel your autonomic response. Find the right place and the right pressure to make this a safe and regulating experience. Listen to the story that comes with this touch.

Other suggestions to explore self-touch include holding your neck and imagining you're connecting with the place where your social engagement system originates, or placing one hand on your heart and the other hand on your face and remembering the actions of the face/heart connection. Try crossing your arms and offering yourself a hug or holding your hands or placing your hands in a prayer or *namaste* position. Experiment with ways of touching your legs and feet. Some touches will feel nourishing, others will be neutral, and still others will feel uncomfortable. Take time to explore different ways of touching. See which ones bring you a flavor of the sympathetic or dorsal states and which ones deepen your ventral experience. Use what you've learned about how your autonomic nervous system is drained and filled to find your way.

Finally, we can add mirrored touch to self-touch. In a mirrored touch moment, you and another person engage in the same self-touch. One person offers and the other person follows. Then you exchange roles. Sometimes mirrored touch brings a deepening of the experience and a closer sense of connection and at other times prompts a move into protection. Two people can feel their systems moving in the same direction or in opposite directions. As you explore mirrored touch, remember there is no right or wrong, there is simply your nervous system's way in this moment.

As we end this chapter, let's reflect on the process of shaping. Shaping happens over time in lots of ways. When we begin our exploration, we don't know which practices will lead us to regulation. We look for lots of ways to practice shaping, so that we have choices to bring the degree of challenge for our system needed in any moment to keep us on the stretch and savor side of the line. Shaping our systems requires persistence to return to practices and patience to let the changes unfold over time. Make the decision to start to shape your system and find practices that you can sustain. Dive into the process and bring qualities of kindness and gentleness with you.

9

Re-Storying

Story makes us more alive, more human,
more courageous, more loving.

MADELEINE L'ENGLE,
THE ROCK THAT IS HIGHER

Through the lens of the nervous system, subtle shifts in our autonomic states and our autonomic patterns translate into new stories
about who we are and how we navigate the world. We humans are
storytellers, meaning-making beings, and it is through our autonomic
nervous systems that we first create, and
then inhabit, our stories. The information that begins in our biology travels
autonomic pathways to the brain, and
the brain creates a story to make sense
of what's happening in the body. As our
biology changes, so do our stories.

> We humans are
> storytellers, meaning-
> making beings, and
> it is through our
> autonomic nervous
> systems that we first
> create, and then
> inhabit, our stories.

Each state brings a different kind of
story. From a dorsal state of shutdown,
the stories are about losing hope, being
lost, or feeling untethered to the world
and to other people. These are stories of
not belonging and being a misfit, unseen and alone. When you touch
into your dorsal survival state, what are the flavors of your stories?

From a sympathetically mobilized state, the stories are about adversar-
ies. We don't care about connection. We have a single focus on survival.

These stories are ones of anger and anxiety, action and chaos. When you tune in and listen to your sympathetic survival state, what stories do you hear?

From the regulation of the ventral state, the stories are ones of possibility and choice. These are stories of connection, of challenges that feel manageable, of feeling safe enough in the world to venture out and explore. As you listen to your ventral state of safety, what stories emerge?

As we learn to befriend the autonomic nervous system, we discover that the stories our system is telling are not rigid or fixed and in fact change over time. When we learn to tune in, we find there are at least three stories always waiting to be heard, one being told from each state. The story that catches our attention and directs our experience comes from the autonomic state that is most active in the moment. When we remember that we have access to more than one story, we can listen with curiosity to each state, begin to interrupt our survival stories, and deepen into stories of safety.

One way to listen to our three stories is to take a particular experience and look at it from each state. I think of this as looking through the eyes of a state. We connect with a state and look out at the world to see what it is like from that perspective. For this exploration we want to choose a small, everyday experience that has just a slight flavor of distress and then travel the hierarchy to look at the experience from each state and listen to each story.

Here is an example from my own life of looking through the eyes of each of my states and feeling one experience in three very different ways. The experience I chose to explore was a moment when I spilled my morning coffee. In this example, notice that the story is a simple one, not totally out of my ordinary experience, and that it doesn't affect my safety or have a big impact in my life. In this exploration, I want to make sure I am first feeling regulated and anchored in ventral safety. Then I begin to dip into dorsal disconnect, and my story becomes *It's not worth trying*. Next, coming up to sympathetic mobilization, the story I hear is *If I only tried harder, worked harder, and paid more attention, I might not be so incompetent*. And finally, looking through the eyes of ventral regulation, the story now transforms to *It's just an accident and not an omen about my day*.

Exploration:
Listening to Three Stories

Now it's your turn. Start by choosing a small, ordinary experience you're curious about and feels just a bit challenging. Before you begin your listening experience, first find your anchor in ventral. Use some of the ways you've learned in prior explorations to feel regulated and ready to safely tune in and listen. (You might return to chapter 2 and revisit your ventral landscape, chapter 6 and the "Connecting with Cues" practice, or chapter 7 and walk your ventral continuum.)

Travel to the dorsal building block at the bottom of the hierarchy. Look through the eyes of your dorsal vagal system and listen for just a moment to the story of your experience from that place. Come up one step on the hierarchy to the sympathetic state. Feel yourself mobilizing with some of that energy. Look through the eyes of your sympathetic nervous system. How do you hear the story of that experience now? Now come back to the ventral state at the top of the hierarchy. Anchor there, look through the eyes of the ventral system, and listen to the story.

Notice how each state brings a very different story. How does hearing your three stories affect your experience? This quick listening practice offers an easy way to bring our different stories into awareness and remember that we don't have to stay stuck in one state and its story.

Building the skill of listening to autonomic stories supports the next move into exploration of re-storying. As we gently shape our systems in new ways and deepen into the nourishing patterns of connection, we move into a time of re-storying. This is a time of bringing attention to the subtle autonomic shifts that are happening and weaving them into a new narrative. We tell stories and hear stories in many different ways, including through art, movement, and words, and we each have our preferred ways to take in, create, and share stories.

I love words. Using words and playing with words feels safe and connecting to me. Movement is a much more challenging experience, often bringing a flavor of disconnection as my dorsal system comes to life, and creating art can bring a similar autonomic response. I've surveyed friends and colleagues and find it's a common experience to have our preferred pathways. Think about the categories of art, movement, and words and feel what your autonomic nervous system response is. Rather than listening to your brain and the cognitive story it tells, see if you can let your nervous system be your guide. What does your autonomic nervous system tell you are your preferred ways to take in, create, and share stories, and what are the pathways that feel a bit challenging?

Whichever pathways we choose, we can experiment with listening, make a small change, and then listen again to hear how the story has been shaped in a new way. I'm going to offer you ways to explore using movement, images, and words. If one of these categories feels too much for you right now, return and explore it later. Staying in the stretch and savor experience is important. Honoring your autonomic wisdom is essential.

Exploration: Moving with Story

Movement is a way we experience our states of protection and connection, and the stories that emerge from our states each have their own rhythms. Whether we enact a movement or it comes to life only in our imagination, movement is a pathway to shaping a new story.

Shifting Patterns

To start this exploration, return to a memory of a moment when you were pulled into dorsal shutdown or sympathetic mobilization and look for a movement to represent that pattern of protection. Find a way of moving that portrays the sense of being caught in that state of survival, unable to find a way out. This can be a partial- or full-body movement (see my example in "Getting Unstuck" below). Begin by just imagining the movement. As you imagine the movement, your autonomic nervous system will feel it, and your motor cortex will join in the experience and begin to bring it to life for you. Imagine your movement and feel what it's like to be stuck in that pattern. Now try enacting the movement. Either sit or stand and bring the movement to life. If this feels too much for you or takes you too deeply into the experience, and you cross the line from stretch to stress, return to imagining the movement. If making the movement feels safe and manageable, carry out the action and feel how your body brings you into the experience of this pattern of protection. Listen to what your nervous system is saying as you hear the story that's brought to life in this particular way of moving.

Now make just a small change to the pattern. Either do this in your imagination or with an action. Change the movement and settle into the new pattern. Where does the small change take you? Listen to the story that accompanies that shift. If the change shifted you out of protection and into a feeling of connection and the beginning of a new story of hope, stay with that new movement and feel its rhythm. If the change didn't quite bring you out of your pattern of protection and the story that's held there, try another small change to the movement.

Experiment until you come to a place where you feel the stirring of change and possibility. Listen to the beginnings of the new story. Using the new movement that brings you into connection, experiment with moving between the old and new patterns. Feel the difference in your body and notice the shift in your state. Take in the experience of being able to flexibly transition between states. As you feel the difference in your body and notice the shift in state, listen to the story that emerges as you move between these patterns.

Getting Unstuck

Sometimes we are stuck in a pattern of protection that we can't seem to move out of. When that happens, movement is a safe way to explore the experience of being stuck, create a new pattern, and invite the beginning of a new story. Begin your exploration by finding a pattern of movement that represents your sense of being stuck. Imagine or enact the movement and see what images and feelings emerge. Listen to the story that is held in the repeating pattern.

Now change the movement in a way that releases you from the pattern. Notice what happens to the image, feelings, and story as you go from being stuck to getting unstuck. Finally move between the two and feel how your state changes as you travel between stuck and unstuck.

Here is my example of being stuck and getting unstuck. My first movement was a cycle of stepping forward and back, forward and back. I imagined myself in that pattern and saw myself on a path stuck in that unending cycle. I felt the hopelessness of having no way out. I stood up as if I was actually walking on that pathway and as I repeated that endless forward-and-back movement, I listened to the story of being trapped, powerless to move forward. And then I simply took a step off the path. I stopped the forward-and-backward motion and stepped to the side. I stepped out of the pattern and stood still for a moment, taking in the feeling of no longer being on my old, well-worn pathway. Then I experimented with moving between the forward-and-back pattern and the simple movement of stepping to the side. I repeated the sequence a few times to feel the change in my body and notice the change in my state. I began to hear the beginnings of a different story in which I was no longer powerless.

Deepening a Pattern of Connection

Movement can also help us anchor more deeply in connection. Bring to mind a moment when you felt anchored in the ventral state and create a movement pattern that represents that state of connection, regulation, and safety. Find a movement that brings alive a sense of flow and possibility. Just like your movement in protection, this could be a partial- or full-body movement. As your nervous system anchors in that movement, sense your motor cortex join in the experience, and feel it come alive. Settle into the repeating rhythm of the pattern. Now, see if you can bring the movement out of imagining into enacting. Again, if this feels too much for you and begins to take you out of stretch into stress, return to imagining the movement. However you connect with this way of moving, let your body bring you the experience of being held in this pattern of connection.

Now make a small change to the pattern. Look for a change that deepens the experience and play with small changes until you've reached the place that feels just right. Listen to the story of well-being this movement brings to life. And now reenact your movement sequence, feel the deepening that takes place as you go from one movement to the other, and listen to the story that emerges from this experience.

Exploration:
Imagining a New Story

Imagery facilitates perception and evokes powerful messages. Even a short one-minute imagery experience has an impact on our autonomic nervous system.[1] This exploration uses our understanding of how the nervous system is shaped and the power of imagery to create a new story.

Follow these basic steps to imagine a new story:

1. Connect with a state of protection or connection.

2. Create an image to represent the state.

3. Listen to the story the image is showing you.

4. Change the image by adding or taking away one small element.

5. Stop and see what happens with your experience and story.

6. Repeat the process until you feel you have reached the point where you have stretched enough and any more would take you into stress.

7. Rest here in the new image and listen to the new story.

8. Spend a moment savoring.

When you are exploring a state of protection, either sympathetic mobilization or dorsal shutdown, the goal is to make subtle changes to the image so the story that emerges is one that takes you toward safety and connection. When you are exploring a state of connection, the goal is to make subtle changes to the image to deepen your story of safety.

Here is a recent example of my own exploration of a dorsal place of disconnection that follows the steps to imagine a new story. My image began with a scene that was barren, with nothing alive, the only colors shades of gray. The story that accompanied the image was of being invisible in an unwelcoming world. The first thing I added was a hint of color with some subtle shades of blues. The story shifted just a bit from a world that was unwelcoming to a world that was asleep. I added a small green plant that was just beginning to sprout, and the story changed again. Now there was a sense of life stirring and it seemed like the world was beginning to wake up. I stopped here, feeling this was the right degree of stretching and any more would move me into stress.

Try this exploration yourself. Begin by connecting with a moment of protection or connection and bring it to life through an image. Add color, sounds, smells, a sense of energy, and any other elements that complete the image. When you feel the image is fully formed, listen to the story.

Now, make a small change to the image. Change one detail, one thing that might bring just a bit of regulating energy in. What's the story now? Take a moment to listen.

Change one more detail and listen in again. How has the story changed now? Continue to play with changing one small detail and listening to the new story. Remember this process of creating a new story is about stretching and not stressing. Stop when you feel you've reached the edge of stretching and reflect on the ways your story has changed. Deepen the re-storying process by adding a moment of savoring practice:

1. Attend: Focus on the new image and story.

2. Appreciate: Feel the richness of the images and words.

3. Amplify: Stay in the experience for up to thirty seconds.

Exploration: Stories with Words

Language is an essential part of what makes us human. The words we choose can help us move out of a pattern of protection and enhance our experiences of safety and connection. Changing just a word or two can have a powerful impact on the state of our nervous system.

We can explore using words to shape our states and stories with a simple three-step process:

1. Write a sentence that illustrates a belief about protection or connection.

2. Change the sentence in some small way by replacing a word, taking a word out, or adding a word in. For a belief about protection, explore changes that shift the belief in the direction of connection. For example, "Relationships are dangerous, and I'm better off on my own," could be rewritten as "*Some* relationships are dangerous, and *sometimes* I'm better off on my own."

For a belief about connection, explore changes that move the belief into a deeper sense of connection. For example, "I'm anchored in my state of safety and connection" might become "I'm *firmly* anchored in my state of safety and connection."

3. Reflect on what happens to your state and your story with the changes.

Try this practice now.

Start by writing a sentence that describes a dorsal-flavored state of protection. Change a word(s) and write a new sentence that shifts the meaning toward the possibility of connection. With your new sentence, reflect on what happens to your state and your story. Repeat the practice by writing a sentence that brings alive a sympathetically charged state of protection. Now change a word(s) and write the new sentence. Remember, you're looking for words that shift the belief in the direction of connection. Reflect on how this affects your state and story. Finish by writing a sentence inspired by a belief about safety in connection. Change a word(s) and write a new sentence that deepens the experience. Reflect on how this changes your state and reshapes your story.

In the simple practice of changing just a word or two, we can listen to the beginnings of a new story.

The Experience of Being Between

The word *chaos* comes from the Greek word *khaos* meaning "empty space" or "the space that exists before things come into being." Re-storying is a process of becoming that requires us to navigate the vulnerability of being in the space between. We're no longer stuck in an old story but not yet grounded in a new one. We're like the trapeze artist in midflight who has let go of one bar and is flying through space reaching for the next bar. When we move into the space between, we take a leap of faith and reach for what comes next. I've come to know this process well over my lifetime, making many leaps and landings. Stop for a moment and think of some of the leaps you've made in your lifetime. Like mine, some have probably had softer landings than others.

Exploration: Leaps and Landings

I'm sure we each have many more leaps and landings to make. To help guide this process, we can follow four steps to the new story: (1) observing where I am now, (2) letting go, (3) taking a leap, and (4) landing safely.

Observing Where I Am Now

Start by thinking of a pattern you're in that feels like it isn't nourishing your nervous system, a pattern that comes from a survival state. Take time to be with this awareness and get to know how this pattern of protection works. Use your journal to document the things you want to note about what you find.

Letting Go

Begin to consider what it would be like to let go of your pattern. Imagine stepping out of that pattern. As you see yourself doing that, look for your worries by filling in the sentence, "If I stepped out of this pattern, then _____." Repeat this a few times until you feel like you have a full understanding of the worries that might get in the way. Having identified the worries, use the same sentence, "If I stepped out of this pattern, then _____" to find the hope. Again, use this sentence several times to feel the ways hope can support you in letting go. End by noticing what happens in your nervous system as you imagine letting go.

Taking a Leap

Take the information you've gathered so far and imagine actually taking one step out of your familiar pattern into the unknown.

You might only see the first step on a stairway or see a bridge and not know where it leads. Or perhaps you might see yourself as a trapeze artist flying through air. As you imagine making a leap, remember you don't know yet where you're heading; you just know you're ready to step out of an old adaptive survival pattern. Bring in just enough regulating, ventral vagal energy to support moving forward and then see yourself taking the leap that will lead you to somewhere new but not yet known. Use your journal to document the experience of taking that leap.

Landing Safely

Finally, see yourself landing in new territory. You don't need to see all the elements of this new place. Feel your ventral vagal system holding you in safety and welcome the curiosity that comes along with that. It's okay to be in this place of not knowing. Look around this new place where you've landed and document what you find.

Now go back and review what you found in each of the four steps. Feel the states and state shifts and the ways you are stretching your system throughout the story. Are there enough cues of safety for you to imagine following through? You can always go back and revisit the leap and landing steps and add some elements that bring more connection to ventral regulation. Return to this four-step process whenever you recognize you're in a re-storying process and moving into the space between, or use the steps as a resource as you begin to consider making a leap.

I'd like to end this chapter with a story about change. Woven into the writing you'll find the four steps of the "Leaps and Landings" exploration, glimmers in the rays of sunshine, and the power of predictable co-regulation (the animals) to create the safety needed to move into a new story.

The Journey

Once a long time ago a young woman set out on a journey. Like all the women in her family, she carried a heavy canoe on her back as she walked. The path was rocky and many times she felt like giving up. Each time she decided she couldn't go on, a tiny ray of sunshine would reach her and warm her heart just a little. Finally she came to the banks of a roaring river. It looked dangerous and impossible to cross, but on the other side she could just make out a beautiful green field. If I can only reach the field, she thought, I can safely rest.

The young woman bravely launched the canoe and was swept into the current. She struggled mightily but was not strong enough to fight the river. She let herself be taken by the current and was carried downstream for many miles until finally she grabbed the branch of a tree hanging over the riverbed. She clung to the branch while she gathered enough strength to pull herself and the canoe out of the river. Resting on the banks of the river, she huddled under the canoe for protection. She knew she couldn't remain under the canoe forever, and she wanted to see the world on this side of the river. So the woman again put the canoe on her back and began to walk. As she walked up hills and through valleys, she met many friendly animals and they asked her why she was carrying a canoe. She said that was what the women in her family did and that she had needed it to cross the river.

The animals told her there were no more rivers in this part of the country and that she would be better able to explore without the heavy canoe on her back. The young woman put the canoe down and tried traveling a few steps without it, but each time she picked it up again. She just couldn't imagine being without it. It felt so strange to not carry that heavy load.

Many miles passed and the young woman reached a mountain. The promise of a beautiful meadow filled with flowers was on the other side. But how could she climb the mountain with a canoe on her back? Could she trust the animals who told her she wouldn't need that canoe again? Could she even imagine a life without carrying the canoe on her back? The animals sat with her and waited while she thought.

She had traveled so far, and it had been such a difficult journey. She wanted so much to reach the meadow. The animals had stayed with her from the moment she first found them. Perhaps she really could trust they would be with her and believe what they were telling her. Maybe she really didn't need the canoe any longer. Maybe it was time to leave it behind. It would always be a part of her memory, but she knew she couldn't take it with her up the mountain.

The young woman cried as she put the canoe down. She had tried so many times before. Would this time be any different? The tiny rays of sunshine that had warmed her heart had now grown into a beam of sunlight. She had her animal friends to travel with her. She knew climbing the mountain would be hard, but she had already escaped the raging river and survived so much. The young woman touched the canoe one last time and then turned away to face the mountain, and she and her animal companions began to climb.

10

Self-Transcendent Experiences

So at the end of this day we give thanks for
being betrothed to the unknown.

JOHN O'DONOHUE,
TO BLESS THE SPACE BETWEEN US

The word *transcendent* comes from the Latin *scandere*, meaning to climb, and the prefix *trans*, meaning beyond. A self-transcendent experience takes us beyond the ordinary and transports us across a boundary. In these moments, we move beyond our singular self into a deep sense of interconnection. We feel a sense of oneness with people and the planet. These are commonly experienced moments no matter what our culture or where we live. Self-transcendent experiences of awe, gratitude, compassion, elevation, and stillness all have their roots in the autonomic nervous system. When we understand how the autonomic nervous system is involved in these powerful moments, we can take them in more fully and create the conditions that support ongoing connection to moments of transcendence.[1]

Awe Filled

A feeling of awe brings a sense of wonder and stimulates our curiosity, taking us out of our everyday life and into a moment of reverence or deep appreciation. In a moment of awe we feel a ventral-inspired connection first to ourselves and then outward to others, the world, and spirit. Some of the benefits of awe include a desire to explore the physical world, an increased interest in reaching out and helping others, a reduction of physical inflammation, and a greater sense of well-being.[2]

In a moment of awe we experience being in the presence of something vast that transforms our experience of the world. We feel both small and connected to something much larger than ourselves, and our old way of thinking no longer fits. We are humbled by our place in the world and filled with wonder. Even our experience of time changes from concrete and limited to expansive and timeless. Awe in its first awakening is a solitary experience, making it available to all of us even when we are on our own either by choice or through circumstance. It is after we take in the moment by ourselves that we are then often moved to reach out and share our experience with others.

Awe is found in extraordinary moments. We encounter something that stops us in our tracks, a moment so awe-inspiring we are awestruck. I experienced a moment like that when I stood in the center of the circle of stones at Stonehenge. Can you remember a moment when you were awestruck? Awe is also found in everyday experiences: a bird singing, a flower blooming in the garden, a piece of music playing. Moments of awe are abundant in our everyday world. How do you recognize them? Be on the lookout for wonder, amazement, or reverence.

> Moments of awe are truly an autonomic-shaping experience.

We are drawn to the places where we experience awe. They become our awe environments. These are the places we can return to easily and predictably find a moment of awe. I live on the coast, and one of my awe environments is walking by the ocean. Another is standing outside before dawn, looking up at the stars and then again seeing the first light in the sky. In these simple moments, in places that are within my reach, I connect to the awesomeness of daily living. Where is a place you can return to easily and find a moment of awe? Look for a place in the natural world where you can feel that you are one being connected to a community of beings and connected to the planet. Once you find an awe environment, you can begin to regularly invite awe into your life.

Just as the nervous system is shaped in small moments that are repeated over time, it seems that small moments of awe add up and predict well-being in the future. Moments of awe are truly autonomic-shaping experiences. Make an intention to connect with awe each day. The awe intention I wrote recently was, "Each morning when I get up, I'll go outside and find the Big Dipper." Write an intention to connect with the everyday moments of awe that are all around you.

A Feeling of Gratitude

Gratitude can be thought of as an appreciation for what is valuable and meaningful to us. It is an experience of thankfulness. Gratitude is both an embodied feeling and an action we take, and, like awe, gratitude is tied to the ventral vagal system. Physically, as we enter a moment of gratitude, our heart rhythms change, our blood pressure drops, our immune function improves, our stress is reduced, and we sleep longer and deeper. Psychologically, we feel more joyful, more alive, more generous, more compassionate, and more connected to others. We experience more life satisfaction and less burnout.[3] These physical and psychological experiences are outcomes of being anchored in the ventral state.

Gratitude is an experience of connection. It is an emotion that exists in relationship with others and that pulls us to want to deepen those relationships. We become aware of receiving goodness and aware that those gifts of goodness come from another human being. When we feel gratitude, we then are moved to want to offer a gift of goodness in return. Gratitude brings the elements of reciprocity alive in our connection with others and creates a positive feedback loop. Reflect on a moment of gratitude. Feel the sense of reciprocity and the flow of ventral energy in the experience of offering and receiving goodness.

We can engage in a multitude of gratitude practices from counting blessings to keeping a gratitude journal, praying, or saying a simple thank you to someone. What all gratitude practices have in common is that they emerge from a ventral vagal state of safety and the nervous system's pull toward connection. When I think about gratitude practices, I think about the ripple effect that comes from throwing a stone in the water. One moment of gratitude, one simple act of goodness, ripples out to reach others one by one, mirroring the circles of ventral vagal connections moving through the world.

Paying It Forward

Elevation may not be a term that you are familiar with, but it is an experience you have likely had many times in your lifetime. Elevation is the inspiring feeling we experience when we see unexpected acts of human goodness, kindness, courage, or compassion. When we are moved in this way, we have the dual response of wanting to help others and wanting to become a better person ourselves. Looking at this response through the lens of the autonomic nervous system, the experience of elevation activates both ventral and sympathetic circuits.[4] The sympathetic system brings mobilizing energy while the ventral system, through the actions of the vagal brake, brings regulation and infuses our actions with compassion. We are touched by an experience and then moved to offer an act of kindness to another person. Through elevation, when we see a good deed, we want to become a doer of good deeds.[5]

Opportunities to experience moments of elevation are all around us. We're moved by news stories that show someone doing a good deed. Accounts of people doing remarkable things pull us to want to do something good ourselves. Remember a time when you were moved in this way, a moment when you experienced elevation. How were you affected by that experience, and what were you moved to do next? Unexpected acts of goodness, kindness, courage, or compassion happen all around us, often without us stopping to notice. Just like a gratitude practice, elevation sends ripples out into the world, changing it one act at a time. However, rather than inspiring us to respond directly to the act we witnessed, elevation stirs us to reach out into the world and pay it forward. Write an intention that will help you be open to seeing acts of goodness, be a witness to goodness, and then become a doer of good deeds.

Compassionate Connections

Archbishop Desmond Tutu once wrote, "We are each made for goodness, love, and compassion. Our lives are transformed as much as the world is when we live with these truths." If empathy is feeling someone's suffering, then a way to think about compassion is empathy in action. I see your suffering, I feel your suffering, and then I'm moved to want to help in some way. Compassion combines an emotional response with a desire to help. And just as we are wired to be in connection with each other, we are wired with an impulse to help, with an instinct for compassion. Research has shown that compassion is part of our human nature. Both giving compassion and receiving compassion have benefits for our well-being. We experience a reduced risk of heart disease, we have a strengthened immune response, and we have an increased resilience to stress.[6]

Remember a time when you felt compassion, when you felt someone suffering and were moved to want to help. As you revisit this moment, feel the energy of your ventral vagal system. And now remember a time when you received a compassionate gesture from someone and again feel the energy of your ventral vagal system. The ventral vagus is an integral part of the experience of offering and receiving compassion. Because of this, the vagus is sometimes called the compassion nerve. If we're chronically in a state of sympathetic mobilization or dorsal vagal collapse, we lose our capacity for compassion. It's only when we're held in the energy of connection, when we're anchored in our ventral vagal system, that we have the capacity for compassion. Only then can we see someone suffering, feel their suffering, be with them, and reach out to offer support.

> If we're chronically in a state of sympathetic mobilization or dorsal vagal collapse, we lose our capacity for compassion.

We can develop a greater capacity for compassion. One of the ways we do this is to strengthen our capacity to be in a state of ventral vagal regulation. All of the practices in the prior sections that help you anchor in the ventral system also support your capacity for compassion. Setting an intention for compassion is a way to resource that capacity. Remembering that compassion is only possible when we're in a ventral vagal state, find your way to your ventral home and anchor there. From that place of safety and connection, write your compassion intention. A practice of creating compassion intentions increases our capacity for compassion, so regularly write a new intention.

When we look through the eyes of compassion, we are able to see someone who is struggling and not make a moral judgment about them. They are not bad or broken; they are stuck in an adaptive survival state. We understand their autonomic nervous system has taken them out of connection into protection, and we can feel compassion for that experience. We have experienced what it's like to be hijacked by a state.

Realizing that we all have a nervous system that is fundamentally wired in the same way is a starting point to developing compassion toward the family and friends around us who at times challenge our capacity for connection, and for the people in the world who think and feel and act in ways unlike ours. Recognizing our commonalities is a foundation for compassion. The compassion practice below, "Just Like Me," is a useful way to bring this awareness into action.

Exploration:
Just Like Me

This practice helps us move from a sense of "me" to a sense of "we" by using statements that recognize not our differences but our similarities. Someone else has a body, a mind, feelings, thoughts, has suffered and experienced joy, and wants to be healthy and feel loved, just like me.

We can take this practice and use it to see how other autonomic nervous systems are ordered and organized and activate in ways just like ours. Imagine these phrases are about a friend and notice what happens for you as you read them.

Just like me, this person experiences times of connection and times of protection.

Just like me, this person responds to cues of safety and cues of danger.

Just like me, this person can disconnect and disappear.

Just like me, this person can feel dangerous.

Just like me, this person can be warm and welcoming.

Take a moment and reflect on these phrases and your autonomic responses. What were your states? What were your stories?

Now imagine these phrases are about someone who is not your friend, who you don't feel connected to, or who you may even have a conflict with.

Just like me, this person experiences times of connection and times of protection.

Just like me, this person responds to cues of safety and cues of danger.

Just like me, this person can disconnect and disappear.

Just like me, this person can feel dangerous.

Just like me, this person can be warm and welcoming.

What happened this time? What states did you experience and what stories did you hear?

Next, write phrases of your own that recognize the natural ways we all regulate, move into survival responses, rest in a state of connection, and can be pulled into protection. Write four or five phrases choosing the autonomic similarities that you want to recognize. Use your phrases and imagine saying them about someone you're close to. Read each phrase and hold this person in your awareness. Notice your autonomic response and the stories that emerge. Now choose someone who is not a friend and read your phrases with that person in mind. Notice how your nervous system responds and the stories that emerge.

Return to this practice often. You can write new statements to deepen your connection with people you're close to and explore how it might feel to connect with people you're struggling with.

The autonomic nervous system is the common denominator in our human experience. It allows us to see others as we are ourselves. Our capacity for compassion is grounded in our capacity to be in a state of ventral vagal regulation and can increase with time and practice. As our ability to anchor in the ventral system deepens, so will our capacity for compassion.

Forgiveness

Compassion has a natural partner in forgiveness. With compassion, it is possible to see beyond the harm someone did to us and see their humanity. Compassion opens the door to moving into forgiveness. Forgiveness is not forgetting; it is remembering from a state of ventral vagal regulation. When we remain unforgiving, our autonomic nervous system holds on to the experience with an activated sympathetic survival state. Remembering brings the experience alive again not just in our minds but also in our biology. We benefit from the autonomic protection of forgiveness and suffer with the autonomic risks of unforgiveness. Offering and receiving forgiveness are both tied to a regulated nervous system.[7] Forgiveness is associated with decreased anxiety and depression and lower rates of cardiovascular disease. When we stay in a state of unforgiving, remembering the harm we suffered or thinking about the person who harmed us activates our sympathetic survival.[8] When we move into forgiveness, we interrupt the autonomic dysregulation that accompanies unforgiving.

Think about being in the state of unforgiveness with someone and imagine you and that person are holding two ends of a toxic rope. Notice how your body responds to this image. This connection keeps you from finding your way back to your anchor in regulation. Now imagine putting down your end of the toxic rope. Take yourself out of that unforgiving connection. As you look at the other person, remember they are still holding their end of the toxic rope and need to do their own work to forgive or make amends and receive forgiveness. See if you feel the emergence of compassion and a beginning ability to forgive. Just imagining forgiving begins the move toward well-being. Even if the thought of moving from unforgiveness to forgiveness feels like too big a leap in this moment, hold on to the thought that in the future it will be possible for you to find your way to the benefits of forgiveness.

Safely Still

While stillness may not ordinarily be thought of as a self-transcendent experience, I include it in this chapter because I believe it takes us out of our ordinary experience to a place of feeling a deep sense of connection. Eckhart Tolle in *The Power of Now* writes, "In the stillness of your presence, you can feel your own formless and timeless reality . . . You look beyond the veil of form and separation. This is the realization of oneness."

The ability to become still without stimulating a survival response is a complicated and challenging process. This excerpt from the poem "After a Blizzard" by poet Gary Whited puts words to the struggle many of us have to hold on to a moment of stillness.

> In this arc of snow
>
> now hanging over the creekbank
>
> in the windless air,
>
> a stillness so silent and at rest
>
> I could not hold it

We again turn to the nervous system to begin to explore coming into stillness. Biologically, stillness is a blend of autonomic states where the two branches of the vagus, the oldest dorsal and newest ventral, work together so we can immobilize without fear. The ventral state brings us alive and into connection with passion, ease, and calm, while the dorsal state brings survival through numbing and collapse. It's only when these two vagal pathways—the ancient energy of immobilization and the new energy of connection—join together that we can experience becoming safely still.

Exploration:
Finding Stillness

When we experience safety in stillness, we can be comfortable with silence, engage in self-reflection, attune with another person and meet them in wordless connection, and be present to the joy of intimate experiences. We each have our own way to describe the experience of stillness. It might be quiet, solitude, or presence. Find the words that fit for you.

Explore your experiences with stillness. Write a stillness statement that creates a drop into dorsal collapse, one that brings a surge of sympathetic energy, and one that invites safe connection with a moment of quiet. For example: "If I become still, I disappear. Stillness is scary, and I need to stay away from it. When I enter into a moment of stillness, the feeling of quiet nourishes me."

For each of us there are certain people and relationships that invite sitting in companionable silence and connecting in stillness. Is there someone in your life with whom you feel safe to be still? Reflect on what it is about that relationship that creates the conditions of safety necessary to share a moment of stillness.

Certain places in our daily lives bring us the opportunity to safely enter into a moment of quiet. Identify the qualities of a place that invite you into stillness. Consider whether you're drawn to a place that is quiet or offers certain sounds. It could be a place where you can be alone or a place where you are with others, an indoor space or outside in nature. Listen to your autonomic nervous system as you explore environments that offer an opportunity for stillness. Look for a place that is easy to return to and where you can regularly find a moment of stillness.

We all have certain times when we can most easily find stillness. Sometimes it's a certain time of day or day of the week.

Sometimes stillness appears when we're engaging in an activity that offers it naturally. Look around your daily living and see if you can find those invitations.

Finally, it's necessary to know when we are in need of a moment of stillness. For this we need to tune in and listen to the cues our autonomic nervous systems are sending. As you think about your personal needs for stillness, what signs suggest that you are longing for a moment of quiet or solitude?

When you know the people, places, and times that offer you opportunities to become safely still and the signs that let you know you need a moment of solitude, you have the information necessary to create a plan to add moments of stillness to your life. Through the practice of coming into stillness, you begin to shape your system in new ways, and your capacity to become safely still deepens. Each moment of stillness is a moment that nourishes your nervous system.

Benevolence

Benevolence fits well with the transcendent experiences we've explored in this chapter. In the dictionary, benevolence is defined as an act of kindness. In our autonomic exploration, benevolence is the active, ongoing, intentional use of ventral vagal energy in service of healing. I'd like to end this chapter by offering you my benevolence meditation from my book *The Polyvagal Theory in Therapy*.

Benevolence Meditation

Make the turn from outward awareness to inner connection. Find the place inside your body where you sense the stirring of ventral vagal energy. This may be in your heart, your chest, your face, behind your eyes, or somewhere else unique to your system. Feel the place where your energy of kindness is born and settle into that space for a moment. Join in the flow of ventral vagal energy as it moves throughout your body.

Maybe there's a sense of warmth spreading. Perhaps your heart feels as if it's expanding or your chest feels full. There might be a tingling in your eyes or a tightness in your throat.

Take a moment to get to know your own personal experience of this ventral vagal flow. Stop and savor this state.

And now imagine using this energy in the service of healing. Feel the power of this state to hold another person or another system in care and compassion. Visualize the many ways you can actively use this state to shape the world. Maybe you're holding a loved one in your stream of ventral vagal energy to ease their suffering. Or perhaps you're the person with an enlivened ventral vagal system in the midst of dysregulation. Take a moment to recognize the people in your life and the places in your world that are in need of your ventral vagal presence. Imagine moving into those connections from your state of ventral vagal abundance.

Through the active, ongoing, intentional offering of ventral vagal energy, you are a beacon of kindness, generosity, goodness, compassion, friendship, and common humanity. Create an intention to beam benevolence.

11

Caring for the
Nervous System

We all have the seeds of love in us.
THICH NHAT HANH

Up until this point we've been exploring how the autonomic nervous
system works and how to begin to shape it in new ways toward
safety and connection. In this chapter we shift from attending to tending
and look at ways to nourish our nervous system. Knowing what nourishes
us and taking actions to connect with those things is part of the ongoing
experience of well-being that is possible when we are anchored in ventral.

Tuning In, Taking In, Tending To

One of the ways we nourish our nervous system is with the steps
of tuning in, taking in, and tending to. Tuning in and taking in are
experiences of connecting and listening while tending to uses an
accompanying action that is based on what we learn from connecting
and listening. We make an intention to tune in to what's happening
in our system not only to notice a move into survival but also to recognize when we're safely anchored in ventral. We listen to what our
neuroception is saying, take in the cues of safety and danger, and see
what's needed to find our way to regulation or deepen the experience
of being anchored in safety. And finally we tend to the needs that are
present by taking an action. Try doing this now:

Tune in: Notice what state you are in. Tune in to the flavor of that state.

Take in: What are the cues of safety and danger you find? What information is your neuroception sending?

Tend to: With the information you now have, what action can you take that will move you toward the safety and regulation of your ventral system or help you anchor more deeply there? What does your nervous system need to feel nourished in this moment?

Through the simple steps of tuning in, taking in, and tending to, we gather the information needed to create a nourishing action. Make an intention to practice this regularly. When setting intentions, it is necessary to find the right degree of challenge for the nervous system. We often have a desire to do something new but set unrealistic expectations about following through. When our brains are not on the same page as our autonomic nervous systems, our intentions can create cues of danger and shut down our ability to engage instead of creating cues of safety and stretching the system.

Set an intention that brings the right degree of challenge. When you think about engaging with this practice, how often do you think you should do it when you first start out? Once an hour? Three times a day? Once a day? Once a week? Write your intention and then read it and see how your nervous system responds. Do you find a ventral vagal inspired "yes," a sympathetic sense that it's too much and brings anxiety and pushback, or a dorsal sense that it's unrealistic, which triggers a loss of hope? When we make an intention and set a goal for our practice without making an agreement that includes our autonomic nervous system, we often don't follow through—not because we don't want to, but because our biology doesn't support it.

Review your plan and revise it in any way needed to support your intention. Write your intention in partnership with your nervous system to create a plan that stays on the stretch side of the stretch-to-stress continuum. Remember, once we cross over the midpoint to the stress side, our system closes to change. When the connection/protection equation tilts more toward cues of danger than safety, we are unable to follow through.

With your new plan to tune in, take in, and tend to that you've created through this brain-body collaboration, see if you are able to follow your intention. Your intention needs to catch, and keep, your interest. As the challenges in our daily lives ebb and flow so does our capacity to engage with a practice. Track your ability to follow through and revisit and revise your intention to fit your changing experience. As you go forward with any intention setting, use this process to find and follow the right degree of challenge for your nervous system.

Flexibility and Resilience

Flexibility and resilience go hand in hand. A flexible system is a resilient system, and a resilient system is a flexible system. We need to remember that well-being is not defined by a nervous system that is always in regulation. A nervous system that brings qualities of well-being still dysregulates, but rather than remaining stuck in a survival response, it finds its way back to regulation through flexibility and resilience. What have you already experienced today? Think about the big shifts that took you from state to state and the more nuanced moves that happened within one state. Take a moment to reflect on the autonomic journey that has brought you to this moment in time.

> We need to remember that well-being is not defined by a nervous system that is always in regulation.

As we nourish our nervous system and create more capacity for ventral vagal energy, we react, return to regulation, and reflect on the experience. Try these three steps with a moment from your day.

1. React: Bring up a moment that had some intensity for you. Consider how you reacted. Where did your nervous system take you?

2. Return to regulation: Remember the feeling of coming back to regulation and anchoring there.

3. Reflect: Take some time to look back on the experience. What is there to learn from the way your nervous system responded?

If we look at resilience through the lens of the autonomic nervous system, we can look at the qualities of frequency (how often we are pulled out of connection into protection), intensity (how strong the survival response is), and duration (how long we are held in sympathetic or dorsal states before we find our way back to ventral regulation). We need to remember that our level of resilience is not stable; it ebbs and flows depending on our physical health, the number of demands we're trying to meet, and the amount of social support and social connection we have.

Exploration: A Continuum of Resilience

A resilience continuum is a good way to track our levels of resilience. To create your continuum you'll need paper and pens or markers. Decide what type of line you want to use. Experiment with vertical lines, horizontal lines, and lines that curve in their own directions. Draw a series of lines to see which one feels right for this exploration. If you have access to markers, choose a color to draw the line for your continuum and then other colors to mark the points along the way.

To begin, label the two ends of your resilience continuum. One end is where you feel an absence of resilience and the other end is where you feel an abundance of resilience. For example, these could be "no energy and no interest" for absence and "resilient and ready" for abundance. Take a moment to find your words.

Now identify several points between the ends. You need enough information to be able to find your place and general level of resilience, so three is probably the minimum number of points needed to track your resilience accurately. You may find more points are easy to identify and useful as you begin to attend. Take some time and name your places.

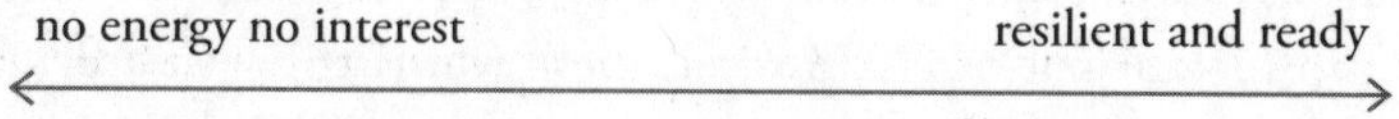

no energy no interest   resilient and ready

<——>

Image 11.1 A resilience continuum

Now find your place on your completed continuum. Where are you today? What is your level of resilience in this moment?

Tracking resilience is an ongoing activity. How resilient we feel guides how we respond to the challenges in our daily life, and the number and kinds of challenges and resources in our daily life impact our capacity for resilience. Create a practice of turning to your continuum and checking in. When we know where we are on our resilience continuum, we have a better understanding of why we are thinking, feeling, and acting in certain ways and a guide to taking the next steps in caring for our nervous system.

Self-Care

For many of us, the concept of self-care is challenging. Practicing self-care is often confused with being selfish. If we look through the lens of the nervous system, self-care is based in ventral vagal safety and connection while being selfish emerges from a survival state. When we are selfish, we're trying to meet a need that comes from a place of fear. Take a moment to see what your nervous system has to say about self-care practices. Listen to your nervous system and fill in the following sentences:

When I'm in my dorsal state of collapse and disconnection, self-care _____.

When I'm in a state of sympathetic mobilization, self-care _____.

When I'm anchored in a ventral state, self-care _____.

For example, when I'm in a dorsal state I might say self-care doesn't enter my thoughts or is out of reach, when I'm in a sympathetic state self-care is a waste of time or will get in the way, and when I'm in a ventral state self-care is an essential ingredient for health and brings me joy.

Saying "should" or "shouldn't" to ourselves is common when we begin to look at self-care. However, these words transmit a demand, not an invitation, a cue of danger not a needed and nourishing message. For instance, "You should exercise, meditate, and go out with friends. You shouldn't eat junk food, watch so much TV, or spend so much time by yourself." Listen for the times you hear yourself saying "should" or "shouldn't" and stop to notice what state is active and what is underneath that demand.

When self-care is guided by the autonomic nervous system, there are two essential questions to consider: "What does my nervous system need in this moment?" and "Is what I'm doing nourishing my nervous system?" Attending to these two questions is the foundation for creating sustainable, autonomically sensitive self-care practices.

Self-care emerges from the variety of options found in our ventral system. Rather than being a rigid routine, autonomically informed self-care includes a menu of choices. Some days your autonomic nervous system will be filled with energy with a vagal brake that has relaxed to allow energy in, and other times you will feel the more restful energies of your ventral system. We need a variety of self-care activities so that each day we have something to engage in that meets our changing needs for autonomic nourishment.

Our individual beliefs about self-care are influenced by the people and places that are a part of our daily lives. Do people around you encourage you to practice self-care, or do they think self-care is unimportant? Do you live in a place where it's easy to practice self-care? Do you work in a place that encourages self-care? If we're surrounded by people who have a rigid view about what constitutes self-care and live and work in places that don't value self-care, we may find it harder to hear and follow our own needs. When we're surrounded by people who encourage self-care and live and work in places that value self-care, we find it easier to attend to self-care and create practices that nourish our nervous system.

Exploration:
Self-Care Circle

The self-care circle is one way to begin to create your own autonomically informed self-care practice. Draw a circle on a piece of paper and then divide the circle into four quadrants with the lines extending beyond the circle. Use pens or colored markers to label the four quadrants: physical, relational, mental, and spiritual. The following directions will take you around the circle in a particular order, but you can complete your circle in any order you choose. As you go through the four quadrants, don't worry if some are more filled than others. We often have quadrants with more self-care activities than others. The process for creating your self-care circle is to first work inside the circle, filling in the quadrants with activities you predictably engage in, and then return and work outside the circle, adding activities you'd like to explore in each of the quadrants.

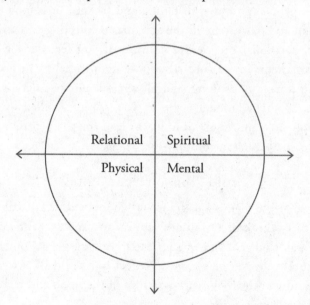

Image 11.2 Self-care circle

Inside the Circle: Physical

Start with the physical quadrant. On the inside of the quadrant, write the things you predictably do in the physical realm for your self-care. As you consider options, ask yourself if the action is a ventral vagal–inspired experience, something that you think you should be doing that has more of a sympathetic need to do it, or a dorsal vagal experience of going through the motions without really caring. As you create your self-care circle, you only want to add activities that truly bring you to a ventral state or deepen your experience there.

Inside the Circle: Relational

Move to the relational quadrant. If you're using markers, choose a different color for this quadrant, and on the inside of the circle, write the things you do with others that are moments of self-care. You might have regular conversations with people, go out with family and friends, or belong to a group and participate in the activities or meetings. In any of your relational experiences consider if you feel filled while doing them. Invite your nervous system to help you decide what a truly nourishing ventral vagal–inspired activity is for you. In this relational realm, if you don't feel filled by the action and connection, or it doesn't lead you to a ventral state, it doesn't belong in your self-care circle.

Inside the Circle: Mental

Move to the mental quadrant and choose a different-colored marker. Think of the things you do to exercise your mind. Do you read? Do you watch certain programs? Do you go to lectures? Do you play games? Reflect on your daily activities and notice which ones are activities of the mind and feel like moments of self-care.

Inside the Circle: Spiritual

End with the spiritual quadrant. Choose a new color of marker. With this category we often think about being connected to something larger than self and finding meaning and purpose in our lives. Look for experiences that take you into a flow of ventral vagal energy and move you into connection with your own definition of what spirit, and spirituality, means to you. Add what you find to your self-care circle.

Take a moment to see how your self-care circle is beginning to take shape. It's not unusual for the same activity to show up in different quadrants. For example, a yoga practice might show up in each of your quadrants: physical in its movement, relational if you do it with others, mental as you exercise your mind in the yoga practice, and spiritual if you feel that connection during your practice. As you look over your circle, notice which quadrants are full and feel nourishing and which ones are in need of attention.

Outside the Circle

The next step is to explore the outside of the circle. Choose colors you haven't used yet to denote the intention to experiment with something new. Start with the physical quadrant and let your nervous system guide you in thinking about what might be fun to explore. Write what you find on the outside of the circle. I encourage you not to edit what you hear. Just because you put something on the outside of the circle doesn't necessarily mean you're going to follow through, but it lets you know that somewhere inside there is a longing to experiment. Then do the same thing with the relational, mental, and spiritual quadrants. What would you like to explore? What appears? What is your nervous system longing for?

Attending to Your Circle

Once you've completed your self-care circle, look at what's on the inside and notice what you're doing now to nourish your nervous system. Look at the things on the outside you've identified as interesting and you feel invited to try. Quadrants that are full point you toward the ways you are tending to your self-care. You might make an intention to spend time exploring a quadrant that is less filled. When we have things in each of our quadrants that we predictably do, we feel a balance in our self-care activities and reap the benefits of autonomic well-being.

The last part of the exercise is to set a time frame for using your self-care circle. It takes a while to settle into building a practice of tending to self-care. Six months is a common time frame, but you might decide that three months or even nine months feels right to you. Write the date you choose on your paper. Keep your self-care circle where you can look at it regularly. Check in with what's on the inside and experiment with what's on the outside.

Your self-care practice is an ongoing, unfolding work in progress. Listen to your nervous system, tend to what is nourishing, and follow what you are curious about. This is not a static activity. Your self-care circle reflects your changing needs and changing practices. When you reach the date you've chosen, do this practice again. See what has changed and create your next self-care circle.

Offering Regulating Energy to Others

When we nourish our nervous system and can anchor in ventral energy, we experience well-being. Even though we get pulled out of regulation into sympathetic and dorsal vagal energies, we know the way home. When we inhabit that place of regulation and navigate our days guided by our ventral vagal system, we not only experience the benefits of well-being but can offer our regulating energy to the people around us. From our anchor in ventral energy, we feel the benefits of our own regulation and are moved to reach out. We take on the responsibility for being a regulating influence for others not as a burden we carry, but as a blessing we can share.

Exploration: Coming into Connection

When we reach out with an offer of connection, we tune in to the autonomic conversations that are happening between systems. Take a moment and think about someone close to you. Look at them through the lens of the autonomic nervous system. How autonomically regulated or dysregulated are they? Are they feeling the safety of connection, or are they caught in a pattern of protection? Take a moment and see if you can sense their system. Bring some curiosity to what their nervous system might need to help them come back into the safety of their own ventral vagal state. How might your regulating presence be helpful?

We know that the nervous system is exquisitely sensitive to the difference between an invitation and a request. Language is one of the ways we feel that difference. We can be moved into a survival response when we hear phrases like "you should" or "you need to" or even "it would be good for you to." "I'm with you" may feel like an invitation to connection, while "I'm here for you" may bring a sense of distance. Experiment with words that bring up a survival response and words that invite connection.

When we are moved to reach out and offer co-regulation, sometimes the choice is to simply be there with another person, and other times a more active way of connecting is needed. The communication between two nervous systems is where we go to find the information to guide our choice. Anchor in the ventral system and be curious about what another nervous system needs. Experiment with ways of offering connection until you find the response that sends cues of safety and an invitation to connect.

The state of the world often seems overwhelmingly dysregulated, and we can be quickly pulled into an adaptive survival state of sympathetic fight and flight or dorsal vagal disconnect and give up. We see this in the responses of the people around us to what's happening in our world and yet, to change the world, to find a way to safety and connection where possibilities emerge, we need ventral energy to light the way. This piece from the poem "Startled by Earth" by my friend and poet Gary Whited speaks to me about the energy of ventral.

> Fresh lit on an early morning
>
> a candle flame offers a voice
>
> so clear, so yellow, so inviting
>
> that I listen.

As we come to the end this chapter, return once more to a practice of self-care. Find the way to your ventral home. Take your time as you travel that familiar pathway. Take in the sights, the sounds, and the sensations along the way. Invite your autonomic nervous system to show you the ways it's being nourished and what it's longing for.

12

Creating Community

When we try to pick out anything by itself, we find
it hitched to everything else in the Universe.

JOHN MUIR

The science of safety and connection is growing each day, and our understanding of how the nervous system works continues to deepen. While
learning about the nervous system can at times feel very scientific, understanding our biology actually opens us up to the mystery and magic of life.
When we are anchored in ventral regulation, there is a feeling of abundance.
We have a sense of being connected to other humans and to the world in
a way that is miraculous. We come to that place of grace in part by understanding the science that shows us the way to anchor in our home in ventral.

The nervous system, with its ever-changing flow of energy that
brings us the many flavors of a state and moves us from state to state,
offers an invitation to go on an autonomic adventure. When we have
the ability to befriend, anchor in ventral energy, and be with our experiences, we listen with interest to the messages our nervous system
sends and are curious about where they might take us. The stronger
our anchor in regulation, the more opportunities we have to take in
the moments of grace, awe, and beauty that we might otherwise miss.
With every heartbeat, with every breath, and in every interaction, our
nervous system is shaping our lives and guiding our experiences. When
we befriend our system and attend to our needs to be nourished, we
bring a ventral vagal–inspired presence as we move through the world.

Profound changes can happen when we are anchored in ventral regulation and begin to live from that place, where there is a sense of trust. We move through the world willing to take a risk, with the belief that when we take a leap we will find a safe landing. When we live from sympathetic mobilization, we don't believe in ourselves or trust that the world will support us in making a change, and when we are in dorsal collapse, we can't even imagine the possibility. When we're in either of these states, we're stuck in a story that is created in our pathways of protection. It's only when we see the world through the eyes of ventral connection that we are able to begin to make different choices about important parts of our lives.

When we have the ability to befriend, anchor in ventral energy, and be with our experiences, we listen with interest to the messages our nervous system sends and are curious about where they might take us.

As we find our way to anchoring in ventral regulation, we begin to experience more physical well-being. With a regulated nervous system, moments of well-being magnify, and some of the old aches and pains and chronic conditions we've lived with begin to change. When we feel an increase in physical well-being, we begin to engage with people and connect with the world in new ways. Often, we first notice simple things like enjoying a meal or having a friendly conversation. Then from this place of paying attention to the small changes that are happening, we begin to notice other, more consequential ways our work to anchor in ventral regulation is making a difference. We are able to stand up for what we believe in and ask for what we need from a place of regulation rather than from a state of protection. We look at the world with compassion and connect with curiosity. We stay out of a story of judgment and understand the people around us not by a label that describes their behaviors but by remembering they are in a state of dysregulation. Our interactions with others are guided by the question, "What does their nervous system need in this moment to feel safe?"

Pathways to Change

In the business world companies create product launch plans to identify the sequence of events that will lead to the successful marketing of a new product. In the world of autonomic reshaping, we can create a plan to support successfully engaging with our personal change process. Think of this as your blueprint to launching a newly shaped nervous system.

Exploration:
Nervous System Launch Plan

When we write our launch plan we begin with a wish. What is it we want to invite in? What leap are we wanting to make? Then we add intention, imagery, writing, and social support to guide our wish into being. The following steps to creating your personal launch plan enlist your autonomic nervous system as an ally. Rather than relying on our brains to lead the way and risk the battle between cognition and capacity, when we invite our nervous system into the process, we ensure that our autonomic state will create the platform needed to support our making the leap and safely landing.

Follow these four steps to creating your personal launch plan:

1. Set the intention: Write your intention. Play with the words and create a statement that catches your interest. Read your statement to yourself and say it out loud. Remember how your nervous system says yes and change the words in any way needed so your system feels fully invested.

2. Create an image: Seeing is believing. Imagery is a thought with sensory qualities. Create a richly detailed picture engaging all of your senses. The following three methods of visualization invite you to see the outcome, the steps, and the challenging places

along the way. Explore each and enlist the nervous system in successfully bringing your intention to life.

- Outcome visualization: Visualizing reaching your goal brings a sense of accomplishment. Outcome visualization engages the ventral vagus in savoring an experience of success.

- Process visualization: Process visualization gets you from *here* to *there*. Staying anchored in ventral regulation, travel the path and see each step along the way.

- Critical visualization: What are the challenges you'll have to navigate? Feel the places where your autonomic nervous system is challenged and where you may need to pay more attention to bringing regulating resources.

3. Write your plan: Bring your intention and visualizations into concrete form. Write your plan in a format that is clear and easy to follow. You might choose to use an outline, write in paragraphs, or illustrate your plan with words and images. Let your autonomic nervous system show you the format that will help you follow your plan.

4. Share your plan: Remembering that the nervous system looks for and longs for connection with others, find someone you want to share your plan with. If you have created a micro-community (described later in this chapter), share your plan there. What does it feel like to tell your plan to someone else? Track your autonomic response. Are you anchored in the ventral state? As you share your plan, are you finding ways you want to change it? Adjust your plan in any way you need to make it a plan that keeps you on the stretch side of the stretch-to-stress continuum.

If the leap you are working on involves an identifiable midway point, it's good to recognize that place in your launch planning. While in our work with continuums we use midpoints to track the ongoing movement back and forth between two places, with a launch plan, the midpoint presents a before-and-after experience. This is the moment when we realize the next step will take us out of the old and into the new.

I recently had the experience of coming to a midpoint and sensing the enormity of that moment. I realized it was my last chance to turn back. The next action would be the turning point and in order to find my way across the midpoint, I had to go back to read my intention and review my written plan to find the reassurance I needed to take the next step. The power of that moment took me by surprise and was a reminder of the importance of attending to midpoints.

There are two places in your launch plan where you can look to add a midway point: (1) in the process visualization as one of the steps along the way and (2) in step 3, when you write your plan, write about crossing the midpoint.

Autonomic Conversations

Deep listening emerges from a place of ventral safety and regulation where our sole intention is to be present and connect, nervous system to nervous system. When we listen without an agenda, without already thinking about how we are going to respond or even how we are going to help, we offer someone the longed for, and often missing, experience of being welcomed, seen, and listened to. We can't enter into this connection and be a witness unless we're anchored in ventral safety, and we don't feel witnessed unless we're with someone who offers that ventral experience to us. To be held in the presence of another is a powerful gift.

Gary Whited shared with me these thoughts about the experience of deep listening:

> Listening, when it opens and we're feeling safe enough, leads toward connection with other people. But it doesn't stop there. It is also the vehicle and the medium for connecting with everything around us. When our listening truly becomes reciprocal, we respond back and forth through call and response within the immense interconnected web we call the universe that surrounds us and holds us always. Our listening opens through numerous portals. We think of it commonly as an auditory phenomenon, yet it passes through other portals as well. We listen with our ears, yes, but we also listen with our eyes, our minds, our hearts, our touch, and upstream from all sensations and perceptions we listen with our autonomic nervous system.

Gary's words are a lovely reminder that, at its core, listening is an autonomic experience. To truly listen we have to be open to connection and feel safe enough to enter into that vulnerable space. Deep listening is only possible when we are anchored in ventral safety. When we know our ventral home and how it feels in all of its manifestations, we can recognize when we're not at home. In order to find our way to listening, we need to be mindful of the moments when we are not in a place of safety and regulation. It's often easy to recognize a state of sympathetic mobilization by the way we feel it in our bodies, the way the energy is felt in the world, and the responses of the people around us. Dorsal disconnect is a little more challenging because rather than being big and taking up space, we disappear, become invisible, and are often overlooked as we move through the world. The explorations in the previous chapters help us recognize when we are home in ventral regulation, notice when we leave home, and help us find our way back to anchor in the state of presence necessary to deeply listen.

The nervous system is a sending-and-receiving hub for information that helps us safely navigate our daily lives. It is at work moment to moment not only inside our own individual systems but in connection with the nervous systems around us. This autonomic conversation is happening within ourselves and between ourselves and others, ourselves and the environment, and ourselves and spirit. In every moment we are transmitting and taking in energy and information. Whether or not we are intentionally connecting with the people around us, we are having an autonomic conversation. As we begin to understand the ways our nervous system impacts the people around us and the places we inhabit, we become aware of our responsibility for the ways we are moving through the world.

Whether in our work world or in our personal lives, the formula is the same. Connection begins with a neuroception of safety. From an anchor in ventral, we are a welcoming, safe presence for the people around us. Other nervous systems feel the energy of safety we are sending and receive an invitation to come into connection. Navigating from a state of protection, we send messages of danger, and other nervous systems heed the warning. It's empowering and also humbling to know that in every moment we are sending and receiving autonomic cues of welcome or warning. When we stop and think about the ways our nervous system is communicating, we understand the importance of attending to the autonomic information we are sending out into the world.

Moments of Missing: Making Repairs

Healthy, nourishing relationships are naturally filled with moments of missing. When we, or the people around us, move out of regulation, misattunement and disconnection happen. These ruptures are a normal and expected part of our relationships, and when they are noticed, named, and repaired, they form a foundation for strong and resilient connections. While we know that rupture and repair is a formula for building healthy relationships, we are not always skillful in the process. To mend our moments of missing, we need to notice the rupture, name it with the other person, and then find the right repair.

Exploration:
Rupture and Repair

When ruptures go unnoticed and unnamed, they linger below the surface of awareness, shaping our relationship stories. To bring these implicit experiences into explicit awareness, we need to know how our nervous system sends a signal that there has been a rupture. Begin to tune in to that by remembering a rupture that was so big it couldn't go unnoticed. How did your nervous system let you know? Then move to a smaller rupture and notice the signals. And finally reflect on a slight misattunement and see how your nervous system conveyed that more subtle message.

Now that you know the signs of rupture, think about a relationship you feel ambivalent about or a person in your life you have a difficult connection with. Are there ruptures that have happened and haven't been recognized? If we notice a rupture but don't name it with the other person, the experience remains unspoken, coloring our story and impacting our relationship. When we get the message of misattunement and don't share it, it sits in our system where it is unavailable for repair and reconnection.

When we notice a rupture, name it, and share it with someone, but don't take the final step of making the repair, we are left feeling the pain of the moment. When we only engage in the first parts of the process, we stay disconnected and feel unseen or unheard. It is when we complete the steps of noticing and naming the rupture and then making the repair that we strengthen the relationship.

The path to repair is guided by our nervous system, so making a repair can take many forms. Finding the repair that mends the rupture is a process of listening and offering and staying in the process until there is a sense of reconnection. Sometimes a heartfelt "I'm sorry" is just right, while other times it's not words but actions that are needed. We may need to engage in a discussion and make a plan to do things differently, or we may simply need an acknowledgment of responsibility and an intention to change. There is no one way to make a repair. There is only the way our nervous system says is the right repair for this rupture.

While it is important to bring awareness to the moment of missing and find the way back into connection, noticing, naming, and repairing don't always happen at the same time. We can notice and name—"It feels like we just moved out of connection"—and then, if we're ready, we can make the repair. We can only make a repair from an anchor in ventral connection, so we may not be regulated enough in the moment of noticing to offer the repair. In those moments we can name the rupture, let the other person know that we're not feeling enough regulation to engage in the next step toward repair, and make a commitment to returning when we are. At other times we're ready to begin the repair, but the person on the other end isn't autonomically available to receive the offer. In those moments we can let the other person know we recognize there has been a rupture and we're available to explore repair when they feel ready.

When we hold moments of missing in our nervous system, they color our connections, and the stories that are created often travel with us from relationship to relationship. The lessons of rupture and repair we learn in one relationship are autonomically, and often automatically, transferred to other relationships. Sometimes the lessons are attached to a certain category—parents, siblings, friends, and colleagues—and other times the lessons are generalized to all relationships. Not only are our relationships impacted in these ways but, when not attended to, the lessons we take in from ruptures that are unrepaired are often passed from generation to generation. My parents' autonomic expectations around ruptures in relationships affect the way they engage with others, and those relationship rules are implicitly passed on to me.

Along with these moments of person-to-person connection, disconnection, and reconnection, we are also continuously engaged in the universal autonomic conversations that naturally occur as we go through our days. When we are anchored in ventral regulation, we send that energy out into the world. In our connections with the people we live with and love, the people we work with, the people in our communities, and the people we simply pass by during the day, our regulated energy has a profound effect. On the days we're not anchored in ventral safety, as we move through the world we broadcast cues of danger. If we're in a sympathetically fueled state of anger or anxiety or a dorsal flavor of just going through the motions but not really being present, the people around us will feel that and have an autonomic response of their own.

As we move through the ebb and flow of regulation, we send messages of welcome or warning out into the world. Even in the moments of casual contact with people during the course of our day, small ruptures happen as our energy of protection is felt. While we can't go back and reconnect with the people we simply passed by in the course of the day and make a repair, the repair we can offer is to notice when we are moving through the day from our home in ventral regulation and bring awareness to intentionally sending out that energy. Rather than a direct person-to-person repair, this is a global offer of safety and connection. Just as our dysregulation sends cues of danger and may start a cascade of other nervous systems moving into protection, so can our being anchored in regulation be enough of a cue to invite other nervous systems to find their way to connection.

Communities of Connection

Our nervous system looks for, and longs for, connection. Throughout our lives we search for opportunities to co-regulate. We receive great physical and psychological benefits from befriending our nervous system and learning to anchor in regulation, and when we share our experiences with others, the benefits magnify. To support our autonomic movement toward well-being, it's helpful to have people in our lives who are willing to share the journey with us. A good place to begin is with a polyvagal partner. Find someone who is curious and wants to explore with you. Look for someone who will help you see what's changing and hear your new stories and who wants you to help them see how they are shaping new pathways as well. Inviting someone to be a polyvagal partner is an opportunity to share what you've learned about your nervous system and help a friend begin to befriend their nervous system. You can share the experience of seeing the world through the lens of the nervous system and listen to each other's autonomic stories. Within this polyvagal partnership there is an invitation to experience deep listening and the intimacy that emerges from this way of being in connection.

> We receive great physical and psychological benefits from befriending our nervous system and learning to anchor in regulation, and when we share our experiences with others, the benefits magnify.

In addition to having a polyvagal partner to accompany us in this process, we benefit from creating a micro-community. Our micro-community is a group of people we intentionally bring together to support us on our reshaping and re-storying journey. These are people we can count on to bring us a ventral welcome, who know our patterns and will celebrate our successes, savor with us when a pattern begins to change, and help us recognize when we are stuck in a pattern of protection. They offer the encouragement we need in just the ways we need it to keep us moving forward. To do this, the people in our micro-communities need to have a basic understanding of how the nervous system works and know the particular patterns of connection and protection our nervous system uses to help us navigate our daily lives.

Exploration:
Creating a Micro-Community
Gathering People

To begin to create your micro-community consider these questions:

> When you think about the people in your life, who would you like to invite to become a part of your micro-community?

> What are the qualities they bring that you feel are important to support your ability to stay anchored in safety as you reshape and re-story?

> Do they already speak the language of the nervous system or do you need to teach them?

> What have you learned about your autonomic pathways that you can share with them?

> What are the signs you want them to know so they can recognize when you have traveled to your home away from home?

Creating the Structure

Once your micro-community is gathered, the next step is to create the structure for engaging with your community members. A micro-community meets our autonomic need for connection and can be utilized in a myriad of ways. Listen to your nervous system and create a plan to engage with the people in your micro-community to gather the support you need to explore new autonomic pathways and embody new stories. There is no one way to structure these connections. The "right" way is the way you create to connect with the people in your micro-community that encourages you to stretch, but not stress, your system. (You can use your stress-to-stretch continuum from chapter 8 to guide your choices.) Your micro-community is there to bring the right degree of challenge so that you feel encouraged to keep taking leaps knowing there will be support for your landings.

To create a structure for your micro-community, consider the following questions:

What are your preferred ways of connecting? When are emails or messages just right, and when do you want to hear someone's voice and see their face?

Which ways of connecting feel organized and nourishing, and which ones feel too structured and confining?

How often do you want to check in with your community?

Share what you've learned with the members of your micro-community.

Bring your Community to Life

With the people you choose to rely on in place and what you now know is necessary for you to safely connect, bring your micro-community to life. There are many ways to launch a micro-community. You might want a celebration to mark the beginning, or a quiet moment to acknowledge the process and appreciate the people. Take time to turn inward. Listen and find the way that feels just right to you.

We connect with one another not just for individual well-being but for the well-being of our human family. Remembering that the nervous system is a common denominator in our human experience and that we are all traveling on the same autonomic highway helps bridge our differences and bring us together. The word *ubuntu* is part of the Zulu phrase *umuntu ngumuntu ngabantu*, which means "a person is a person through other people." It is often translated to mean "I am because we are." Looking through the lens of the nervous system we feel the wisdom of ubuntu in the ways we are wired for connection.

As we end our exploration of communities of connection, we can look toward the forest for inspiration. Trees show us the necessity of connection for survival through what has been called the nervous system of the forest.[1] We have learned how a tree intertwines its roots with another tree and connects to neighboring trees through underground fungal networks of these shared root systems, creating support networks.[2] Like us, trees thrive with community. A single tree is connected beneath the ground to the trees around it, two trees intertwine their roots and grow together, and groves of trees join and reach toward the sky. Come into awareness of the ways you are in community. You can stand alone and know you are connected to others, engage in the reciprocity of a polyvagal partnership, and join with your micro-community. Savor the ways each of these connections nourishes you.

CONCLUSION

To finish the moment, to find the journey's end in every step of
the road, to live the greatest number of good hours, is wisdom.

RALPH WALDO EMERSON,
ESSAYS, LECTURES, AND ORATIONS

Looking through the eyes of the autonomic nervous system, we see
a world of both/and. When we know how our nervous system is
organized, we can both let go of shame and blame and become responsible for the ways we navigate daily living. We are both able to move
out of connection into protection and find our way home to ventral safety. Rather than feeling trapped in a survival state with limited
choices, we have access to curiosity, compassion, and self-compassion,
and daily living takes on a sense of expansion and possibility.

We know ventral vagal energy is the essential ingredient for
well-being and when there is enough ventral energy alive and active
in our system, we can find our way to safety and connection. Ventral
energy is accessible individually within our own systems and in community as we connect with others. Sometimes we find our way home
to ventral safety with self-regulating moments, and other times we need
another person to help us find our anchor. With a menu to choose from,
we can reach for the right resource in the moment. Each time we find
our way, we deepen the pathways of connection.

We are on a quest to become active operators of our nervous system
and skillful at anchoring in ventral regulation. Our nervous system is
shaped and reshaped in every moment. The field of human social
genomics is beginning to show us how the way we perceive our world
impacts our genetic makeup. The cues of safety and danger that we
take in through our neuroception shape our biology.[1] Our nervous

system is engaged in ongoing conversations with others and with the world around us, and those conversations influence our sense of safety and well-being. With every breath our vagal brake is at work. When I stop and consider the energies that are moving beneath the surface of awareness and how they shape my daily experience, I am filled with wonder.

> We are on a quest to become active operators of our nervous system and skillful at anchoring in ventral regulation.

Our journey is one of anchoring in so we can look out in a new way. Our exploration is about our history and how our nervous system responds to our experiences. Seeing the world through the lens of the nervous system is a different way to navigate daily living and is often easier to explore with the companionship of others. As we embrace our biological longing for connection and build a community that speaks the language of the nervous system, we resource our own capacity to navigate in this new way and support others as they explore anchoring in and looking out.

Returning one final time to recognize the power of both/and, when we learn to be responsible for our own regulation and travel the autonomic pathways of connection, we are both shaping our own pathways and shaping the pathways in our global community. It is in the experience of finding our way to being anchored in ventral safety and offering that welcome to others that we begin to change the world one nervous system at a time.

ACKNOWLEDGMENTS

I've always been curious about the ways our bodies and our brains work, both in my clinical work helping people find their way back to safety following traumatic experiences and in finding my own way through the challenges of life. I have a deep desire to understand how we humans are put together. And while I studied neuroscience, and even spent time in a histology lab seeing how the human brain is constructed, discovering Polyvagal Theory changed the work I do and how I understand myself and move through the world. I've had the good fortune to learn from and collaborate with Stephen Porges, and he and I have formed a deep friendship. Steve's brilliant mind and generous spirit are a rare combination, and his presence in my life is a gift.

Writing *Anchored* was a step out of my familiar clinical world and quickly became a both/and experience—both a joy to write for my fellow curious human beings and a challenge to find the words. There were times when I felt like I was talking to a friend and the writing flowed, and other times when no matter how hard I tried, words eluded me. In the moments when writing became too big a challenge and I despaired of finding the words, people predictably showed up to offer me a ventral vagal lifeline. During the many months of working on this project I have been reminded over and over that while I write in solitude, I am held in a network of wise and wonderful people.

I am grateful for my group of colleagues who are my sounding board and whose clinical wisdom helps shape my writing, and for my friends who entrusted me with their stories that help bring the explorations to life. I want to say a special thank you to my friend Gary Whited for sharing his beautiful work and to Anastasia Pellouchoud and Caroline Pincus at Sounds True, who were there to offer support when this project stretched my system. As always, much love to my husband, Bob, who has been by my side in all my writing adventures and reminds me I know the way to my ventral home.

Woven into the pages of *Anchored* is my hope that befriending the nervous system will become a routine part of life and the language of Polyvagal Theory will be spoken in homes everywhere. With deep appreciation for joining me on this ventral vagal–inspired adventure, I'm sending a glimmer to light your way.

—DEB

NOTES

Chapter 3: Learning to Listen

1. Kristin Neff and Christopher K. Germer, *The Mindful Self-Compassion Workbook: A Proven Way to Accept Yourself, Build Inner Strength, and Thrive* (New York: Guilford Press, 2018).

2. Brenda Ueland, "Tell Me More," *Ladies' Home Journal* (November 1941).

3. *Merriam-Webster*, s.v. "listen," accessed August 31, 2020, merriam-webster.com/dictionary/listen.

Chapter 4: The Longing for Connection

1. Theodosius Dobzhansky, *Mankind Evolving* (New Haven: Yale University Press, 1962), 150–52.

2. Marjorie Beeghly and Ed Tronick, "Early Resilience in the Context of Parent-Infant Relationships: A Social Developmental Perspective," *Current Problems in Pediatric and Adolescent Health Care* 41, no. 7 (2011): 197–201, doi.org/10.1016/j.cppeds.2011.02.005.

3. Sebern F. Fisher, *Neurofeedback in the Treatment of Developmental Trauma: Calming the Fear-Driven Brain* (New York: W. W. Norton & Company, 2014).

4. John T. Cacioppo and Stephanie Cacioppo, "Social Relationships and Health: The Toxic Effects of Perceived Social Isolation," *Social and Personality Psychology Compass* 8, no. 2 (2014): 58–72, doi.org/10.1111/spc3.12087.

5. Jenny De Jong Gierveld and Theo Van Tilburg, "The De Jong Gierveld Short Scales for Emotional and Social Loneliness: Tested on Data from 7 Countries in the UN

Generations and Gender Surveys," *European Journal of Ageing* 7, no. 2 (September 2010): 121–30, doi .org/10.1007/s10433-010-0144-6; Jingyi Wang et al., "Associations Between Loneliness and Perceived Social Support and Outcomes of Mental Health Problems: A Systematic Review," *BMC Psychiatry* 18, no. 1 (2018), doi.org/10.1186/s12888-018-1736-5; Adnan Bashir Bhatti and Anwar ul Haq, "The Pathophysiology of Perceived Social Isolation: Effects on Health and Mortality," *Cureus* (2017), doi.org/10.7759/cureus.994.

6. Marinna Guzy, "The Sound of Life: What Is a Soundscape?" Smithsonian Center for Folklife and Cultural Heritage, 2017, folklife.si.edu/talkstory /the-sound-of-life-what-is-a-soundscape.

7. Guzy, "Sound of Life."

8. Alan S. Cowen et al., "Mapping 24 Emotions Conveyed by Brief Human Vocalization," *American Psychologist* 74, no. 6 (2019): 698–712, doi.org/10.1037/amp0000399; Emiliana R. Simon-Thomas et al., "The Voice Conveys Specific Emotions: Evidence from Vocal Burst Displays," *Emotion* 9, no. 6 (2009): 838–46, doi.org/10.1037 /a0017810.

9. Louise C. Hawkley and John T. Cacioppo, "Loneliness Matters: A Theoretical and Empirical Review of Consequences and Mechanisms," *Annals of Behavioral Medicine* 40, no. 2 (2010): 218–27, doi.org/10.1007 /s12160-010-9210-8; John T. Cacioppo and Stephanie Cacioppo, "Social Relationships and Health."

10. John T. Cacioppo, James H. Fowler, and Nicholas A. Christakis, "Alone in the Crowd: The Structure and Spread of Loneliness in a Large Social Network," *Journal of Personality and Social Psychology* 97, no. 6 (2009): 977–91, doi.org/10.1037/a0016076.

11. Mary Elizabeth Hughes et al., "A Short Scale for Measuring Loneliness in Large Surveys," *Research on Aging* 26, no. 6 (2004): 655–72, doi.org /10.1177/0164027504268574.

12. David Steindl-Rast, *May Cause Happiness: A Gratitude Journal* (Boulder, CO: Sounds True, 2018), unnumbered pages (approximately p. 41).

Chapter 7: Anchoring in Safety

1. Ulf Andersson and Kevin J. Tracey, "A New Approach to Rheumatoid Arthritis: Treating Inflammation with Computerized Nerve Stimulation," *Cerebrum: The Dana Forum on Brain Science* (2012): 3; M. Rosas-Ballina et al., "Acetylcholine-Synthesizing T Cells Relay Neural Signals in a Vagus Nerve Circuit," *Science* 334, no. 6052 (2011): 98–101, doi.org/10.1126/science.1209985; Vitor H. Pereira, Isabel Campos, and Nuno Sousa, "The Role of Autonomic Nervous System in Susceptibility and Resilience to Stress," *Current Opinion in Behavioral Sciences* 14 (2017): 102–7, doi.org/10.1016 /j.cobeha.2017.01.003; Rollin McCraty and Maria A. Zayas, "Cardiac Coherence, Self-Regulation, Autonomic Stability, and Psychosocial Well-Being," *Frontiers in Psychology* 5 (2014), doi.org/10.3389 /fpsyg.2014.01090; Stephen W. Porges and Jacek Kolacz, "Neurocardiology Through the Lens of the Polyvagal Theory," in *Neurocardiología: Aspectos Fisiopatológicos e Implicaciones Clínicas*, ed. Ricardo J. Gelpi and Bruno Buchholz (Barcelona: Elsevier, 2018); Jennifer E. Stellar et al., "Affective and Physiological Responses to the Suffering of Others: Compassion and Vagal Activity," *Journal of Personality and Social Psychology* 108, no. 4 (2015): 572–85, doi.org/10.1037/pspi0000010.

2. Bethany E. Kok et al., "How Positive Emotions Build
    Physical Health," *Psychological Science* 24, no. 7 (June
    2013): 1123–32, doi.org/10.1177/0956797612470827.

3. Andrea Sgoifo et al., "Autonomic Dysfunction and Heart
    Rate Variability in Depression," *Stress* 18, no. 3 (April
    2015): 343–52, doi.org/10.3109/10253890.2015
    .1045868; Gail A. Alvares et al., "Reduced Heart Rate
    Variability in Social Anxiety Disorder: Associations with
    Gender and Symptom Severity," *PLOS ONE* 8, no. 7
    (2013), doi.org/10.1371/journal.pone.0070468; Angela
    J. Grippo et al., "Social Isolation Disrupts Autonomic
    Regulation of the Heart and Influences Negative Affective
    Behaviors," *Biological Psychiatry* 62, no. 10 (2007):
    1162–70, doi.org/10.1016/j.biopsych.2007.04.011;
    Bethany E. Kok and Barbara L. Fredrickson, "Upward
    Spirals of the Heart: Autonomic Flexibility, as Indexed
    by Vagal Tone, Reciprocally and Prospectively Predicts
    Positive Emotions and Social Connectedness," *Biological
    Psychology* 85, no. 3 (2010): 432–36, doi.org/10.1016/j
    .biopsycho.2010.09.005; Fay C. M. Geisler et al., "The
    Impact of Heart Rate Variability on Subjective Well-
    Being Is Mediated by Emotion Regulation," *Personality
    and Individual Differences* 49, no. 7 (2010): 723–28,
    doi.org/10.1016/j.paid.2010.06.015.

4. Fred B. Bryant, Erica D. Chadwick, and Katharina
    Kluwe, "Understanding the Processes That Regulate
    Positive Emotional Experience: Unsolved Problems and
    Future Directions for Theory and Research on Savoring,"
    International Journal of Wellbeing 1, no. 1 (2011), doi
    .org/10.5502/ijw.v1i1.18; Paul E. Jose, Bee T. Lim, and
    Fred B. Bryant, "Does Savoring Increase Happiness?
    A Daily Diary Study," *Journal of Positive Psychology* 7, no.
    3 (2012): 176–87, doi.org/10.1080/17439760.2012
    .671345; Jennifer L. Smith and Fred B. Bryant, "Savoring

and Well-Being: Mapping the Cognitive-Emotional Terrain of the Happy Mind," *The Happy Mind: Cognitive Contributions to Well-Being* (2017): 139–56, doi.org /10.1007/978-3-319-58763-9_8.

Chapter 8: Gentle Shaping

1. Richard P. Brown and Patricia L. Gerbarg, "Sudarshan Kriya Yogic Breathing in the Treatment of Stress, Anxiety, and Depression: Part I—Neurophysiologic Model," *Journal of Alternative and Complementary Medicine* 11, no. 1 (2005): 189–201, doi.org/10.1089/acm.2005.11.189; Ravinder Jerath et al., "Physiology of Long Pranayamic Breathing: Neural Respiratory Elements May Provide a Mechanism That Explains How Slow Deep Breathing Shifts the Autonomic Nervous System," *Medical Hypotheses* 67, no. 3 (2006): 566–71, doi.org/10.1016/j .mehy.2006.02.042; Marc A. Russo, Danielle M. Santarelli, and Dean O'Rourke, "The Physiological Effects of Slow Breathing in the Healthy Human," *Breathe* 13, no. 4 (2017): 298–309, doi.org/10.1183/20734735.009817; Bruno Bordoni et al., "The Influence of Breathing on the Central Nervous System," *Cureus* (January 2018), doi.org/10.7759/cureus.2724.

2. Elke Vlemincx et al., "Respiratory Variability Preceding and Following Sighs: A Resetter Hypothesis," *Biological Psychology* 84, no. 1 (2010): 82–87, doi.org/10.1016/j. biopsycho.2009.09.002; Elke Vlemincx, Ilse Van Diest, and Omer Van den Bergh, "A Sigh Following Sustained Attention and Mental Stress: Effects on Respiratory Variability," *Physiology & Behavior* 107, no. 1 (2012): 1–6, doi.org/10.1016/j.physbeh.2012.05.013; Evgeny G. Vaschillo et al., "The Effects of Sighing on the Cardiovascular System," *Biological Psychology* 106 (2015): 86–95, doi.org/10.1016/j.biopsycho.2015.02.007.

3. India Morrison, Line S. Löken, and Håkan Olausson, "The Skin as a Social Organ," *Experimental Brain Research* 204, no. 3 (2009): 305–14, doi.org/10.1007 /s00221-009-2007-y; Mariana von Mohr, Louise P. Kirsch, and Aikaterini Fotopoulou, "The Soothing Function of Touch: Affective Touch Reduces Feelings of Social Exclusion," *Scientific Reports* 7, no. 1 (2017), doi.org/10.1038/s41598-017-13355-7; Evan L. Ardiel and Catharine H. Rankin, "The Importance of Touch in Development," *Paediatrics & Child Health* 15, no. 3 (2010): 153–56, doi.org/10.1093/pch/15.3.153; Tiffany Field, "Touch for Socioemotional and Physical Well-Being: A Review," *Developmental Review* 30, no. 4 (2010): 367–83, doi.org/10.1016/j.dr.2011.01.001; Chigusa Yachi, Taichi Hitomi, and Hajime Yamaguchi, "Two Experiments on the Psychological and Physiological Effects of Touching—Effect of Touching on the HPA Axis-Related Parts of the Body on Both Healthy and Traumatized Experiment Participants," *Behavioral Sciences* 8, no. 10 (2018): 95, doi.org/10.3390/bs8100095.

4. B. Spitzer and F. Blankenburg, "Stimulus-Dependent EEG Activity Reflects Internal Updating of Tactile Working Memory in Humans," *Proceedings of the National Academy of Sciences* 108, no. 20 (February 2011): 8444–49, doi.org/10.1073/pnas.1104189108; Charité–Universitätsmedizin Berlin, ed., "How a Person Remembers a Touch," ScienceDaily (2011), sciencedaily .com/releases/2011/05/110510101048.htm.

Chapter 9: Re-Storying

1. Muriel A. Hagenaars, Rahele Mesbah, and Henk Cremers, "Mental Imagery Affects Subsequent Automatic Defense Responses," *Frontiers in Psychiatry* 6 (March 2015), doi.org/10.3389/fpsyt.2015.00073.

Chapter 10: Self-Transcendent Experiences

1. Paul K. Piff et al., "Awe, the Small Self, and Prosocial Behavior," *Journal of Personality and Social Psychology* 108, no. 6 (2015): 883–99, doi.org/10.1037/pspi0000018; Sara B. Algoe and Jonathan Haidt, "Witnessing Excellence in Action: The 'Other-Praising' Emotions of Elevation, Gratitude, and Admiration," *Journal of Positive Psychology* 4, no. 2 (2009): 105–27, doi.org/10.1080 /17439760802650519; David Bryce Yaden et al., "The Varieties of Self-Transcendent Experience," *Review of General Psychology* 21, no. 2 (2017): 143–60, doi.org /10.1037/gpr0000102; Dacher Keltner and Jonathan Haidt, "Approaching Awe, a Moral, Spiritual, and Aesthetic Emotion," *Cognition and Emotion* 17, no. 2 (2003): 297–314, doi.org/10.1080/02699930302297.

2. Robert A. Emmons and Robin Stern, "Gratitude as a Psychotherapeutic Intervention," *Journal of Clinical Psychology* 69, no. 8 (2013): 846–55, doi.org/10.1002 /jclp.22020.

3. Walter T. Piper, Laura R. Saslow, and Sarina R. Saturn, "Autonomic and Prefrontal Events During Moral Elevation," *Biological Psychology* 108 (2015): 51–55, doi.org/10.1016/j.biopsycho.2015.03.004.

4. Adam Maxwell Sparks, Daniel M. T. Fessler, and Colin Holbrook, "Elevation, an Emotion for Prosocial Contagion, Is Experienced More Strongly by Those with Greater Expectations of the Cooperativeness of Others," *PLOS ONE* 14, no. 12 (April 2019), doi.org/10.1371 /journal.pone.0226071.

5. James N. Kirby et al., "The Current and Future Role of Heart Rate Variability for Assessing and Training Compassion," *Frontiers in Public Health* 5 (March 2017), doi.org/10.3389/fpubh.2017.00040.

6. Jennifer L. Goetz, Dacher Keltner, and Emiliana Simon-Thomas, "Compassion: An Evolutionary Analysis and Empirical Review," *Psychological Bulletin* 136, no. 3 (2010): 351–74, doi.org/10.1037/a0018807; Jennifer E. Stellar et al., "Affective and Physiological Responses to the Suffering of Others: Compassion and Vagal Activity," *Journal of Personality and Social Psychology* 108, no. 4 (2015): 572–85, doi.org/10.1037/pspi0000010; Peggy A. Hannon et al., "The Soothing Effects of Forgiveness on Victims' and Perpetrators' Blood Pressure," *Personal Relationships* 19, no. 2 (2011): 279–89, doi.org/10.1111/j.1475-6811.2011.01356.x.

7. Charlotte van Oyen Witvliet, Thomas E. Ludwig, and Kelly L. Vander Laan, "Granting Forgiveness or Harboring Grudges: Implications for Emotion, Physiology, and Health," *Psychological Science* 12, no. 2 (2001): 117–23, doi.org/10.1111/1467-9280.00320.

8. Loren Toussaint et al., "Effects of Lifetime Stress Exposure on Mental and Physical Health in Young Adulthood: How Stress Degrades and Forgiveness Protects Health," *Journal of Health Psychology* 21, no. 6 (2014): 1004–14, doi.org/10.1177/1359105314544132; Everett L. Worthington Jr. and Michael Scherer, "Forgiveness Is an Emotion-Focused Coping Strategy That Can Reduce Health Risks and Promote Health Resilience: Theory, Review, and Hypotheses," *Psychology & Health* 19, no. 3 (2004): 385–405, doi.org/10.1080/0887044042000196674; Kathleen A. Lawler et al., "A Change of Heart: Cardiovascular Correlates of Forgiveness in Response to Interpersonal Conflict," *Journal of Behavioral Medicine* 26, no. 5 (2003): 373–93, doi.org/10.1023/a:1025771716686.

Chapter 12: Creating Community

1. Valentina Lagomarsino, "Exploring the Underground Network of Trees—The Nervous System of the Forest," May 6, 2019, sitn.hms.harvard.edu/flash/2019 /exploring-the-underground-network-of-trees-the -nervous-system-of-the-forest/.

2. Diane Toomey, "Exploring How and Why Trees 'Talk' to Each Other," Yale Environment 360, September 1, 2016, e360.yale.edu/features/exploring_how_and_why _trees_talk_to_each_other.

Conclusion

1. G. M. Slavich and S. W. Cole, "The Emerging Field of Human Social Genomics," *Clinical Psychological Science* 1, no. 3 (2013): 331–48.

ABOUT
THE AUTHOR

Deb Dana, LCSW, is a clinician and consultant specializing in using the lens of Polyvagal Theory to understand and resolve the impact of trauma and create ways of working that honor the role of the autonomic nervous system. She developed the Rhythm of Regulation Clinical Training Series and lectures internationally on ways Polyvagal Theory informs work with trauma survivors. She is a founding member of the Polyvagal Institute, clinical advisor to Khiron Clinics, and an advisor to Unyte. Deb's clinical publications include *The Polyvagal Theory in Therapy: Engaging the Rhythm of Regulation*, *Polyvagal Exercises for Safety and Connection: 50 Client-Centered Practices*, *Clinical Applications of Polyvagal Theory: The Emergence of Polyvagal-Informed Therapies* (with Stephen W. Porges), and *Polyvagal Flip Chart*.

Deb is delighted to partner with Sounds True to bring her polyvagal perspective to a general audience through *Befriending Your Nervous System: Looking Through the Lens of Polyvagal Theory* and *Anchored: How to Befriend Your Nervous System Using Polyvagal Theory*.

To learn more, visit rhythmofregulation.com.

ABOUT
SOUNDS TRUE

Sounds True is a multimedia publisher whose mission is to inspire and support personal transformation and spiritual awakening. Founded in 1985 and located in Boulder, Colorado, we work with many of the leading spiritual teachers, thinkers, healers, and visionary artists of our time. We strive with every title to preserve the essential "living wisdom" of the author or artist. It is our goal to create products that not only provide information to a reader or listener but also embody the quality of a wisdom transmission.

For those seeking genuine transformation, Sounds True is your trusted partner. At SoundsTrue.com you will find a wealth of free resources to support your journey, including exclusive weekly audio interviews, free downloads, interactive learning tools, and other special savings on all our titles.

To learn more, please visit SoundsTrue.com/freegifts or call us toll-free at 800.333.9185.

sounds true
WAKING UP THE WORLD